YOU'RE YOU, CHARLIE BROWN

Books by Charles M. Schulz

Peanuts
More Peanuts
Good Grief, More Peanuts!
Good Ol' Charlie Brown
Snoopy
You're Out of Your Mind, Charlie Brown!
But We Love You, Charlie Brown
Peanuts Revisited
Go Fly a Kite, Charlie Brown
Peanuts Every Sunday
It's a Dog's Life, Charlie Brown
You Can't Win, Charlie Brown
Snoopy, Come Home
You Can Do It, Charlie Brown
We're Right Behind You, Charlie Brown
As You Like It, Charlie Brown
Sunday's Fun Day, Charlie Brown
You Need Help, Charlie Brown
Snoopy and the Red Baron
The Unsinkable Charlie Brown
You'll Flip, Charlie Brown
You're Something Else, Charlie Brown
Peanuts Treasury
You're You, Charlie Brown

YOU'RE YOU, CHARLIE BROWN

A NEW PEANUTS® BOOK

by Charles M. Schulz

HOLT, RINEHART AND WINSTON
New York Chicago San Francisco

Published simultaneously in Canada by Holt, Rinehart and Winston of Canada, Limited.

First published in book form in 1968.

Library of Congress Catalog Number: 68-9205

First Edition

8730004

Printed in the United States of America

PSYCHIATRIC HELP 5¢
WINTER RATES 7¢
PSYCHIATRIC HELP 5¢
WINTER RATES 7¢
"WINTER RATES...7¢"
MAY I ASK WHY YOUR RATES GO UP IN THE WINTERTIME?
I DON'T HAVE TO ANSWER THAT QUESTION!
BY GOLLY, WE DOCTORS GET TIRED OF ALL THIS CRITICISM FROM YOU LAYMEN!
WINTER RATES 7¢
IT MAKES US NERVOUS.. WE'RE VERY SENSITIVE, YOU KNOW!
WINTER RATES 7¢
IT TAKES A SENSITIVE PERSON TO BE ABLE TO DO WHAT WE DO... WE CAN'T STAND ALL THIS CONSTANT CRITICISM!
PSYCHIATRIC HELP 5¢
?
WINTER RATES 7¢
WHERE'D HE GO?
WINTER RATES 7¢
STUPID LAYMAN...HE DIDN'T EVEN WISH ME "HAPPY NEW YEAR"!
SCHULZ

HERE'S THE WORLD WAR I FLYING ACE ZOOMING THROUGH THE AIR IN HIS SOPWITH CAMEL
IT'S OUTRAGEOUS HAVING TO FLY A MISSION ON NEW YEAR'S DAY!
WHAT DO THOSE PEOPLE AT HEADQUARTERS THINK WE ARE?
ACTUALLY, I'VE BEEN UP ALL NIGHT DRINKING ROOT BEER!
SCHULZ

THIS IS LEAP YEAR..
SO?
I GUESS MAYBE YOU'RE RIGHT
SCHULZ

THAT'S HIS "HA-HA, YOU HAVE TO SHOVEL IT, AND I DON'T" DANCE!
SCHULZ

NICE GOING...IT TOOK THAT STONE FOUR THOUSAND YEARS TO GET TO SHORE, AND NOW YOU'VE THROWN IT BACK!
EVERYTHING I DO MAKES ME FEEL GUILTY..
SCHULZ

HEY, EVERYBODY! LET'S PLAY "KING OF THE HILL"!
WHOEVER IS ON TOP WILL BE "KING," SEE, AND...
ALL RIGHT, LET'S PLAY "QUEEN OF THE HILL"
SCHULZ

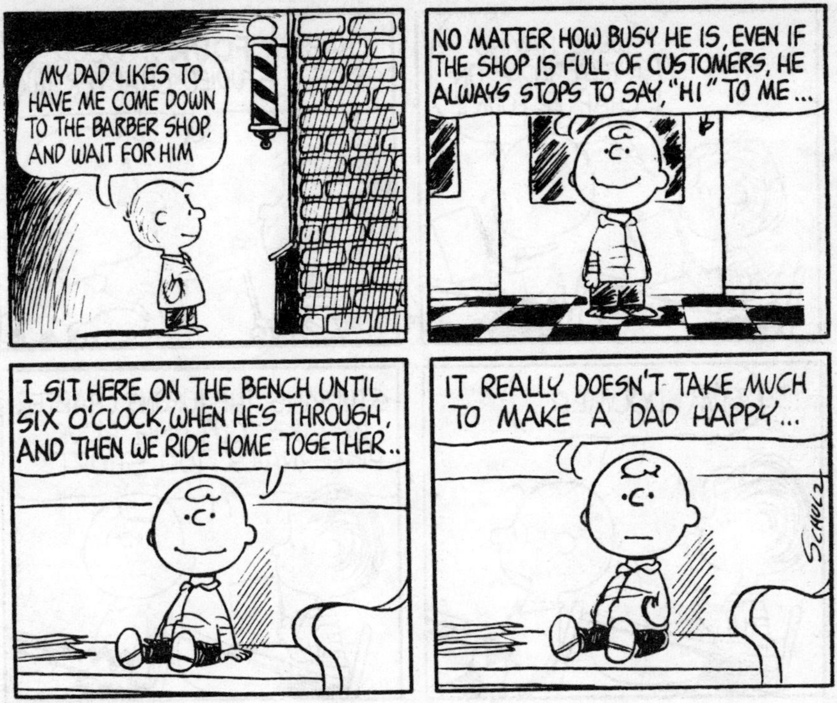
MY DAD LIKES TO HAVE ME COME DOWN TO THE BARBER SHOP, AND WAIT FOR HIM
NO MATTER HOW BUSY HE IS, EVEN IF THE SHOP IS FULL OF CUSTOMERS, HE ALWAYS STOPS TO SAY, "HI" TO ME...
I SIT HERE ON THE BENCH UNTIL SIX O'CLOCK, WHEN HE'S THROUGH, AND THEN WE RIDE HOME TOGETHER..
IT REALLY DOESN'T TAKE MUCH TO MAKE A DAD HAPPY...
SCHULZ

I CAN'T STAND THAT COMMERCIAL!
SCHULZ

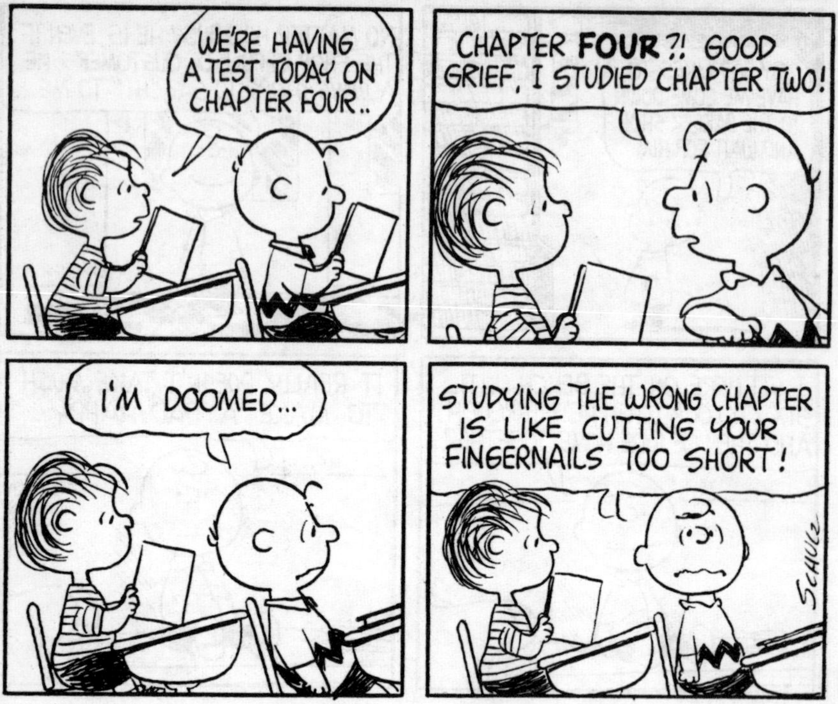
WE'RE HAVING A TEST TODAY ON CHAPTER FOUR..
CHAPTER **FOUR**?! GOOD GRIEF, I STUDIED CHAPTER TWO!
I'M DOOMED...
STUDYING THE WRONG CHAPTER IS LIKE CUTTING YOUR FINGERNAILS TOO SHORT!
SCHULZ

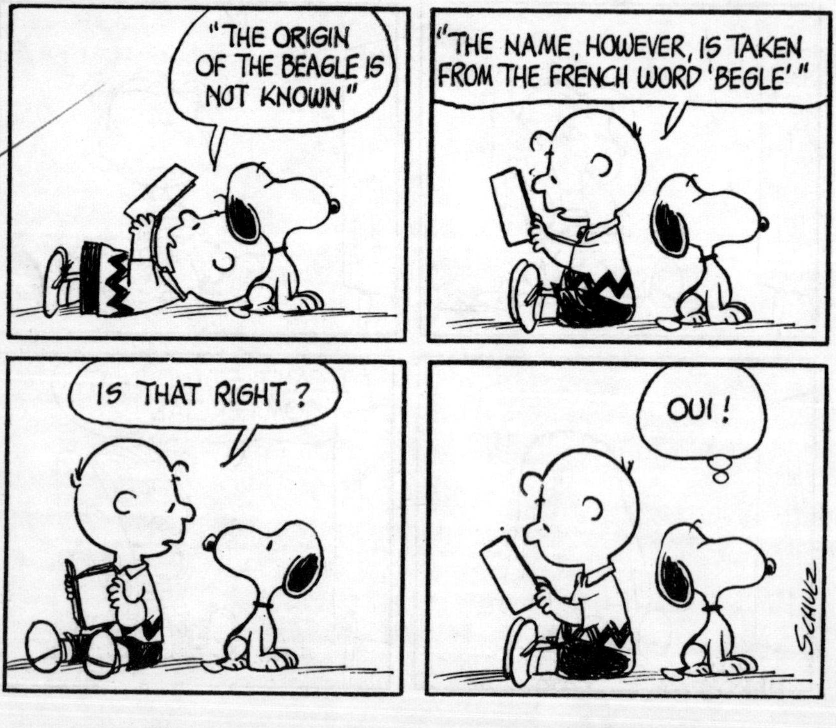
"THE ORIGIN OF THE BEAGLE IS NOT KNOWN"
"THE NAME, HOWEVER, IS TAKEN FROM THE FRENCH WORD 'BEGLE' "
IS THAT RIGHT?
OUI!
SCHULZ

YOU'RE A VERY BORING PERSON, CHARLIE BROWN
YAWN
EXCUSE ME...
I GET BORED JUST TALKING ABOUT HOW BORING YOU ARE..
SCHULZ

THIS KID AT SCHOOL SAID I HAVE A FUNNY FACE...
IS IT ALL RIGHT IF I TELL HIM YOU'RE GOING TO SLUG HIM? YOU CAN BE MY KNIGHT IN SHINING ARMOR...
I'D RATHER YOU DIDN'T
WHAT KIND OF A KNIGHT ARE YOU?
I'M A DOVE KNIGHT
SCHULZ

YOU STUPID KID, YOU THINK YOU'RE SO SMART!
I HAVE A BOY FRIEND WHO'S GOING TO CLOBBER YOU!
I'M NOT YOUR BOY FRIEND, AND I'M NOT GOING TO CLOBBER ANYBODY!
DON'T GO 'WAY! I HAVE TO TALK HIM INTO IT!!
SCHULZ

THIS KID AT SCHOOL INSULTED ME, SEE?
NOW, WHAT I WANT YOU TO DO IS BITE HIM ON THE LEG TO HELP ME GET EVEN WITH HIM..
BITE SOMEONE....JUST TO GET EVEN?
HOW GAUCHE!
SCHULZ

YOU CUT THAT OUT, YOU STUPID DOG!
WHY DON'T YOU GO SOME PLACE ELSE, AND SKATE?
YEAH, YOU'RE A NUISANCE! YOU AND YOUR FANCY FIGURES!
WHY DON'T YOU JUST GET OUT OF HERE?
GO ON! GET OUT OF HERE!
GET OUT OF HERE, AND LEAVE US ALONE!
SCHULZ

PSYCHIATRIC HELP 7¢
OKAY, MAC, WHAT'S YOUR PROBLEM?
THE DOCTOR IS IN
PEOPLE!
PSYCHIATRIC HELP 7¢
I FIND THAT PEOPLE TAKE ADVANTAGE OF ME..
THE DOCTOR IS IN
LIKE IN TALKING, FOR INSTANCE..PEOPLE TALK TO ME ON AND ON, AND I GET BORED AND WANT TO LEAVE, BUT I DON'T, AND THEY KEEP ON AND..
IT'S YOUR OWN FAULT! YOU'RE JUST TOO WISHY-WASHY!
THE DOCTOR IS IN
PEOPLE WHO TALK TOO MUCH DESERVE TO BE INSULTED! THEY DESERVE TO HAVE OTHER PEOPLE WALK AWAY FROM THEM! TALKING TOO MUCH IS AN UNFORGIVABLE SOCIAL SIN! ABSOLUTELY UNFORGIVABLE!
THE DOCTOR
THE ONLY WAY TO DEAL WITH PEOPLE WHO TALK TOO MUCH IS TO LET THEM KNOW JUST HOW BORING THEY REALLY ARE...
THE DOCTOR
YOU CAN'T WASTE YOUR TIME WITH THEM...NO, SIR!
WHY SHOULD YOU SIT AND WASTE YOUR VALUABLE TIME WHILE SOME BORE TALKS ON AND ON ABOUT NOTHING?
THE DOCTOR
LIFE IS TOO SHORT TO WASTE IT LISTENING TO SOME PERSON WHO DOESN'T KNOW WHEN TO SHUT UP! TIME IS TOO VALUABLE! TIME IS...
SIGH!
SCHULZ

YOU'VE BEEN MORE CRABBY THIS YEAR THAN EVER BEFORE!
YOU'VE BEEN CRABBY EVERY DAY! DO YOU REALIZE THAT? DO YOU REALIZE THAT YOU HAVEN'T MISSED A SINGLE DAY?
I WISH YOU HADN'T MENTIONED IT
WHY NOT?
NOW YOU'VE JINXED ME... I WAS GOING FOR A NO-HITTER!
SCHULZ

FIFTEEN SNOWBALLS?
YOU MUST BE KIDDING! THAT'S RIDICULOUS!
BEHIND A TREE, YOU SAY? OH, COME ON NOW!
HOW COULD I POSSIBLY HIDE FIFTEEN SNOWBALLS BEHIND A TREE?
SCHULZ

I DON'T KNOW, I'VE JUST FELT CRABBY EVER SINCE THE YEAR BEGAN
EVERYTHING SEEMS SO HOPELESS... DO YOU FEEL CRABBY, TOO? WHY DON'T YOU COME OVER? SURE, BRING HER ALONG IF SHE FEELS CRABBY... BRING EVERYBODY!
I'M HAVING A "CRAB-IN"!
SCHULZ

HI, GIRLS! WHERE..
GET OUT OF THE WAY!!!
WE'RE ON OUR WAY TO A "CRAB-IN"!
SCHULZ

KNOCK
KNOCK
IS THIS WHERE THE "CRAB-IN" IS BEING HELD?
WHO WANTS TO KNOW?
THIS MUST BE THE PLACE
SCHULZ

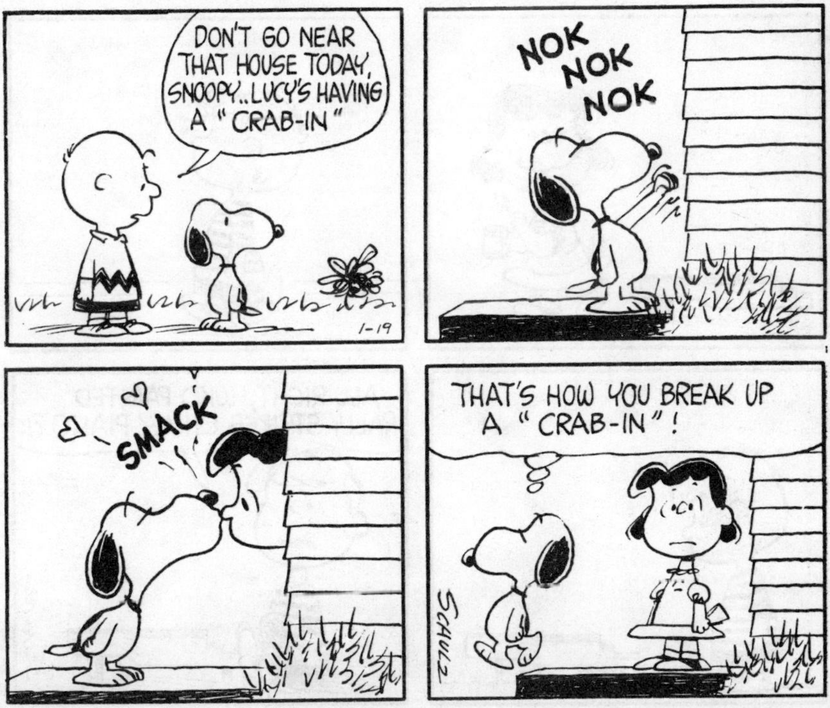
DON'T GO NEAR THAT HOUSE TODAY, SNOOPY.. LUCY'S HAVING A " CRAB-IN "
1-19
NOK
NOK
NOK
SMACK
THAT'S HOW YOU BREAK UP A " CRAB-IN " !
SCHULZ

KER-CHUNK!
THANK YOU VERY MUCH, SNOOPY..
I WAS ALL OUT OF STAMPS
YOU'RE WELCOME
I'M THE ONLY ONE IN THE NEIGHBORHOOD WITH A POSTAGE METER
SCHULZ

ALL RIGHT, WHO PAINTED RALLY STRIPES ON MY PIANO?!
SCHULZ

THE SUN IS GOING TO MELT YOUR SNOWMAN!
THE SUN IS GOING TO MELT YOUR SNOWMAN, AND ALL THAT WORK WILL BE FOR NOTHING! THE SUN IS GOING TO MELT YOUR SNOWMAN!
I SAID THE SUN IS GOING TO MELT THIS SNOWMAN!
STUPID SUN!!
SCHULZ

CHARLIE BROWN, HOW DOES IT FEEL TO KNOW THAT YOU WILL NEVER BE A HERO?
WHAT MAKES YOU THINK I'LL NEVER BE A HERO? I MAY SURPRISE YOU! I MAY SAVE A LIFE OR REPORT A FIRE OR DO ALMOST ANYTHING!
LET ME PUT IT THIS WAY... HOW DOES IT FEEL WAY DOWN DEEP INSIDE IN YOUR VERY HEART OF HEARTS TO KNOW THAT YOU WILL NEVER BE A HERO?
TERRIBLE!
SCHULZ

IF YOU HIT ME WITH THAT SNOWBALL, I'LL **CLOBBER** YOU WITH THIS ONE!
ARE YOU GOING TO LET HER BLUFF YOU THAT WAY?
NEVER TRADE A HIT FOR A CLOBBER!
SCHULZ

HOW IN THE WORLD DO YOU FIND A SNOW-COVERED SUPPER DISH?!
SCHULZ

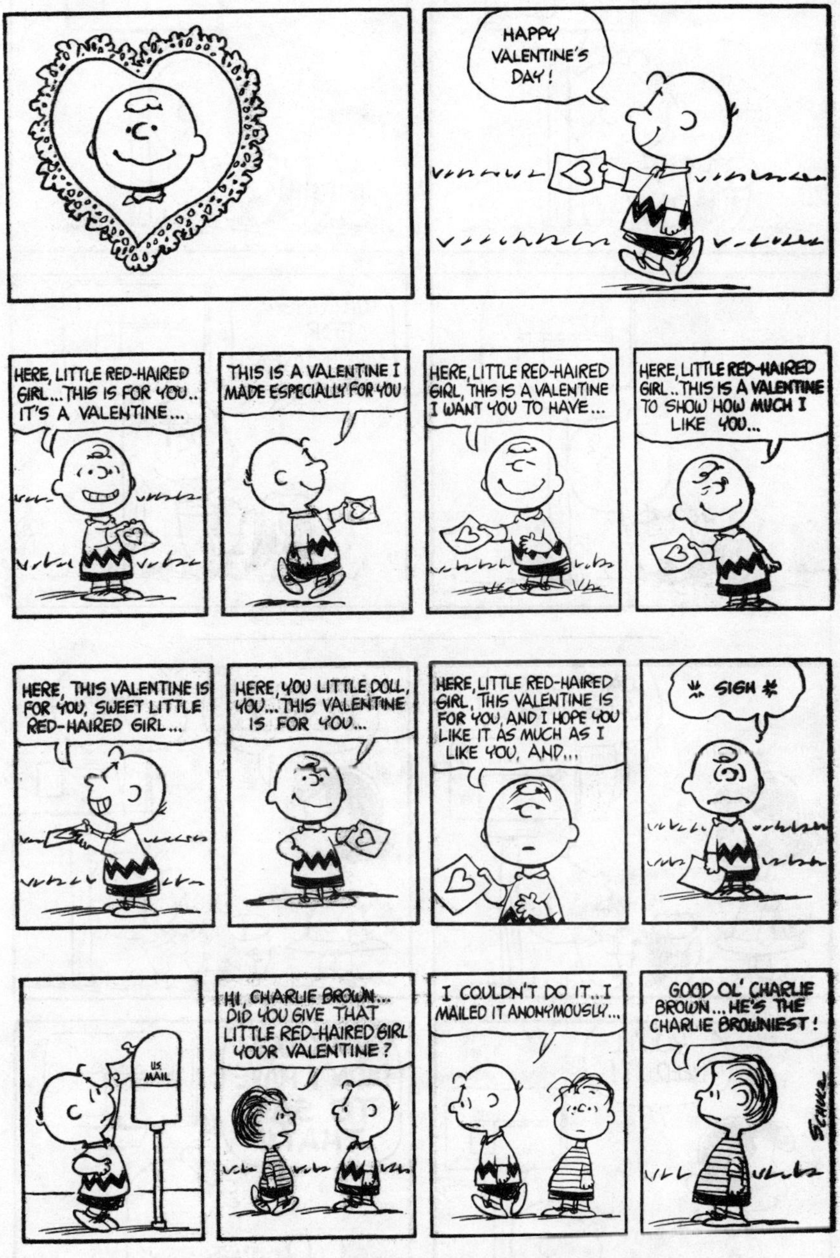
HAPPY VALENTINE'S DAY!
HERE, LITTLE RED-HAIRED GIRL...THIS IS FOR YOU.. IT'S A VALENTINE...
THIS IS A VALENTINE I MADE ESPECIALLY FOR YOU
HERE, LITTLE RED-HAIRED GIRL, THIS IS A VALENTINE I WANT YOU TO HAVE...
HERE, LITTLE RED-HAIRED GIRL..THIS IS A VALENTINE TO SHOW HOW MUCH I LIKE YOU...
HERE, THIS VALENTINE IS FOR YOU, SWEET LITTLE RED-HAIRED GIRL...
HERE, YOU LITTLE DOLL, YOU...THIS VALENTINE IS FOR YOU...
HERE, LITTLE RED-HAIRED GIRL, THIS VALENTINE IS FOR YOU, AND I HOPE YOU LIKE IT AS MUCH AS I LIKE YOU, AND...
SIGH
U.S. MAIL
HI, CHARLIE BROWN... DID YOU GIVE THAT LITTLE RED-HAIRED GIRL YOUR VALENTINE?
I COULDN'T DO IT..I MAILED IT ANONYMOUSLY...
GOOD OL' CHARLIE BROWN... HE'S THE CHARLIE BROWNIEST!
SCHULZ

WAITING FOR VALENTINES!
SCHULZ

WAITING FOR VALENTINES...
OH.....WELL, GOOD LUCK..
THANK YOU
YOU'LL NEED IT!
YOU DIDN'T HAVE TO SAY THAT!!
SCHULZ

SIGH
SCHULZ

AND I GOT A VALENTINE FROM JOYCE AND I GOT ONE FROM PEGGY
AND I GOT ONE FROM ZELMA, AND JANELL, AND BOOTS, AND PAT, AND SYDNEY, AND WINNIE, AND JEAN, AND ROSEMARY, AND COURTNEY, AND FERN, AND MEREDITH ...
AND AMY, AND JILL, AND BETTY, AND MARGE, AND KAY, AND FRIEDA, AND ANNABELLE, AND SUE, AND EVA, AND JUDY, AND RUTH ...
AND BARBARA, AND OL' HELEN, AND ANN, AND JANE, AND DOROTHY, AND MARGARET, AND...
I CAN'T STAND IT... I JUST CAN'T STAND IT...
SCHULZ

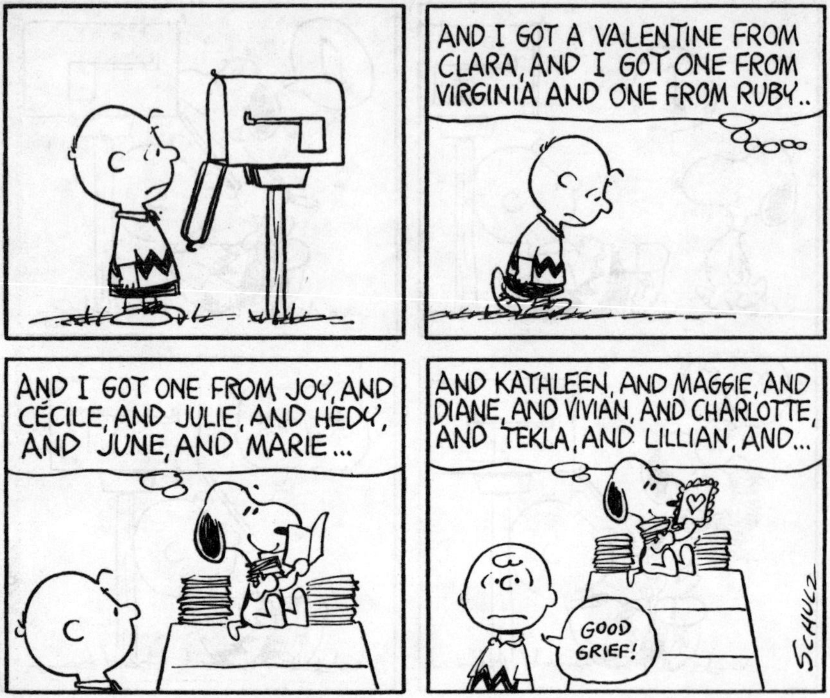
AND I GOT A VALENTINE FROM CLARA, AND I GOT ONE FROM VIRGINIA AND ONE FROM RUBY..
AND I GOT ONE FROM JOY, AND CÉCILE, AND JULIE, AND HEDY, AND JUNE, AND MARIE...
AND KATHLEEN, AND MAGGIE, AND DIANE, AND VIVIAN, AND CHARLOTTE, AND TEKLA, AND LILLIAN, AND...
GOOD GRIEF!
SCHULZ

AND EDNA, AND NAOMI, AND LILA, AND FRAN, AND..
YOU DIDN'T GET A VALENTINE FROM LILA!
I DIDN'T? DIDN'T LILA SEND ME A VALENTINE?
LILA DOESN'T LOVE ME ANY MORE!
OH, WELL... AND CONNIE, AND CHIYO, AND MARILYN, AND AILEEN, AND..
I CAN'T STAND IT... I JUST CAN'T STAND IT....
SCHULZ

ACTUALLY, THEY ALL LOOK ALIKE TO ME!
SCHULZ

OKAY, I'M READY... THROW ME THE HOCKEY BALL!
YOU INVITED HER.. I DIDN'T
SCHULZ

I LOVE PLAYING HOCKEY BALL!
SCHULZ

NOW HERE'S THE WAY WE START THE GAME..
WE HAVE A "FACE-OFF," SEE... WE LEAN OVER AND TAP OUR STICKS TOGETHER THREE TIMES.... OKAY, LET'S GO...
SMAK!
PENALTY BOX
SCHULZ

POOF!
PICK A CARD... ANY CARD..
SCHULZ

I'M DEPRESSED, LINUS...
I NEED AN ENCOURAGING WORD TO CHEER ME UP
HAPPINESS LIES IN OUR DESTINY LIKE A CLOUDLESS SKY BEFORE THE STORMS OF TOMORROW DESTROY THE DREAMS OF YESTERDAY AND LAST WEEK!
I THINK THAT BLANKET IS DOING SOMETHING TO YOU!
SCHULZ

AH! THE SUN'S OUT!
THIS YEAR I'M DETERMINED..
I'M NOT EVEN GOING TO WAIT FOR SUMMER...
THIS YEAR I'M GOING TO START EARLY, AND TRY TO GET A GOOD TAN!
SCHULZ

YOU DON'T UNDERSTAND GIRLS, DO YOU, CHARLIE BROWN?
NO, I GUESS I DON'T...
AND WHEN YOU GROW UP, YOU PROBABLY WON'T UNDERSTAND WOMEN!
SOMEHOW, I THINK THAT'S VERY FUNNY..
I'M HYSTERICAL
SCHULZ

THE EASTER BUNNY IS OUT IN OUR FRONT YARD!
SURE, HE IS..
HE'S HIDING EGGS...HE'S DOING A SPRING DANCE, AND HE'S HIDING EGGS ALL OVER THE FRONT LAWN...
UH HUH... SURE, HE IS...
I THINK I'LL GO OUT AND GATHER UP ALL THE EGGS
WHY DON'T YOU JUST DO THAT...
YOU MISS A LOT WHEN YOU SIT AND WATCH TV ALL DAY LONG...
SCHULZ

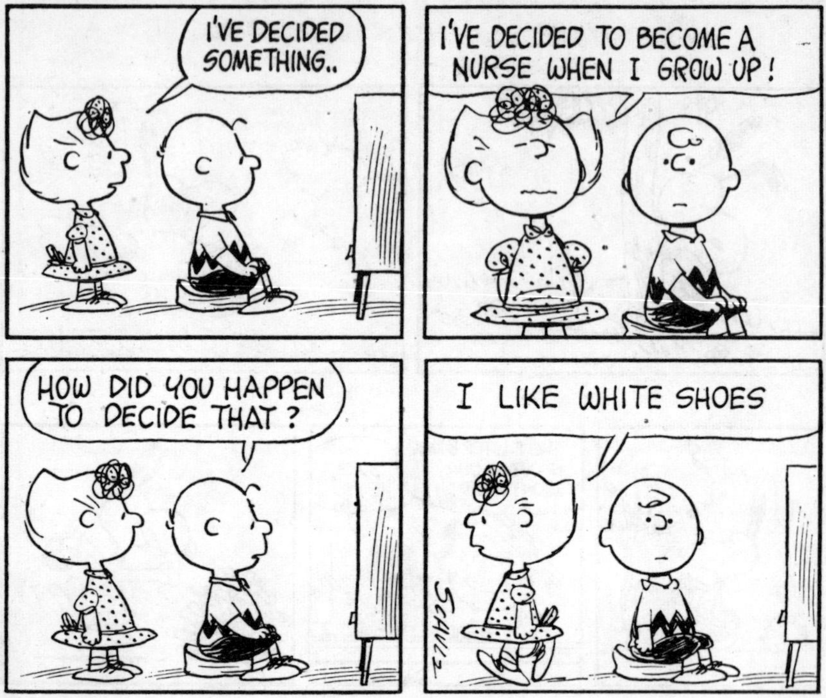
I'VE DECIDED SOMETHING..
I'VE DECIDED TO BECOME A NURSE WHEN I GROW UP!
HOW DID YOU HAPPEN TO DECIDE THAT?
I LIKE WHITE SHOES
SCHULZ

I CAN'T TALK TO THAT LITTLE RED-HAIRED GIRL BECAUSE SHE'S SOMETHING AND I'M NOTHING
IF I WERE SOMETHING AND SHE WERE NOTHING, I COULD TALK TO HER, OR IF SHE WERE SOMETHING AND I WERE SOMETHING, THEN I COULD TALK TO HER...
OR IF SHE WERE NOTHING AND I WERE NOTHING, THEN I ALSO COULD TALK TO HER...BUT SHE'S SOMETHING AND I'M NOTHING SO I CAN'T TALK TO HER...
FOR A NOTHING, CHARLIE BROWN, YOU'RE REALLY SOMETHING!
SCHULZ

I WONDER IF I WOULDN'T BE MORE POPULAR IF I HAD A NEW NAME...
THE WRONG NAME CAN BE A REAL HINDRANCE TO A PERSON'S FUNCTIONING IN SOCIETY.. I THINK A NAME WHICH IS CONSISTENT WITH A PERSON'S PERSONALITY IS IMPORTANT
I WONDER WHAT WOULD BE A GOOD NAME FOR ME...
HOW ABOUT "SUPERMOUTH"?
I'VE GOT TO STOP THIS BUSINESS OF TALKING WITHOUT THINKING...
SCHULZ

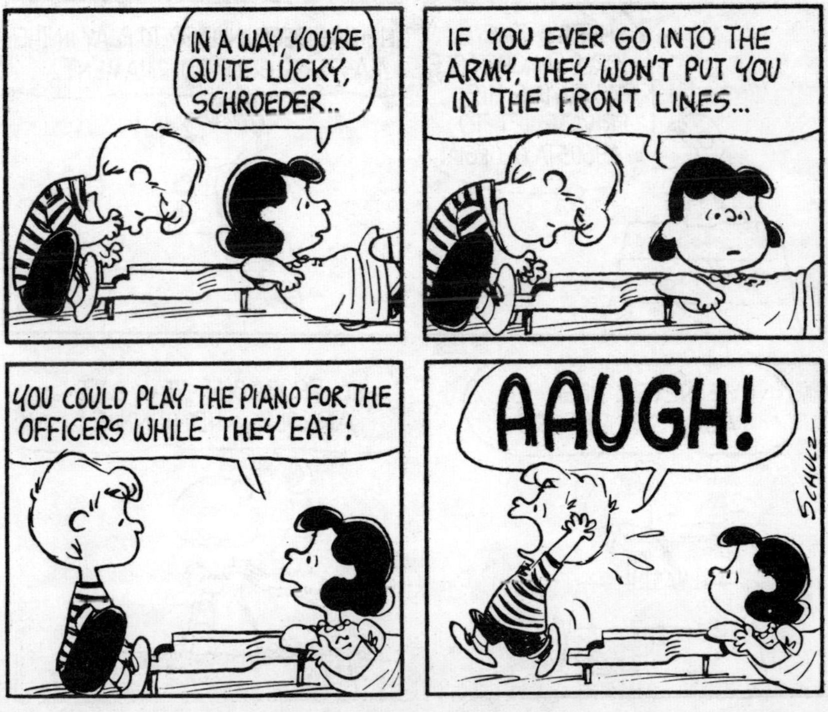
IN A WAY, YOU'RE QUITE LUCKY, SCHROEDER..
IF YOU EVER GO INTO THE ARMY, THEY WON'T PUT YOU IN THE FRONT LINES...
YOU COULD PLAY THE PIANO FOR THE OFFICERS WHILE THEY EAT!
AAUGH!
SCHULZ

HERE'S THE WORLD FAMOUS GOLF-PRO RECEIVING HIS INVITATION TO PLAY IN THE MASTERS
AH, WHAT A THRILL !! GEORGIA IN THE SPRING!
I CAN SEE MYSELF NOW STANDING ON THE FIRST TEE...
ACTUALLY, BEAGLES ARE ALMOST NEVER INVITED TO PLAY IN THE MASTERS...
SCHULZ

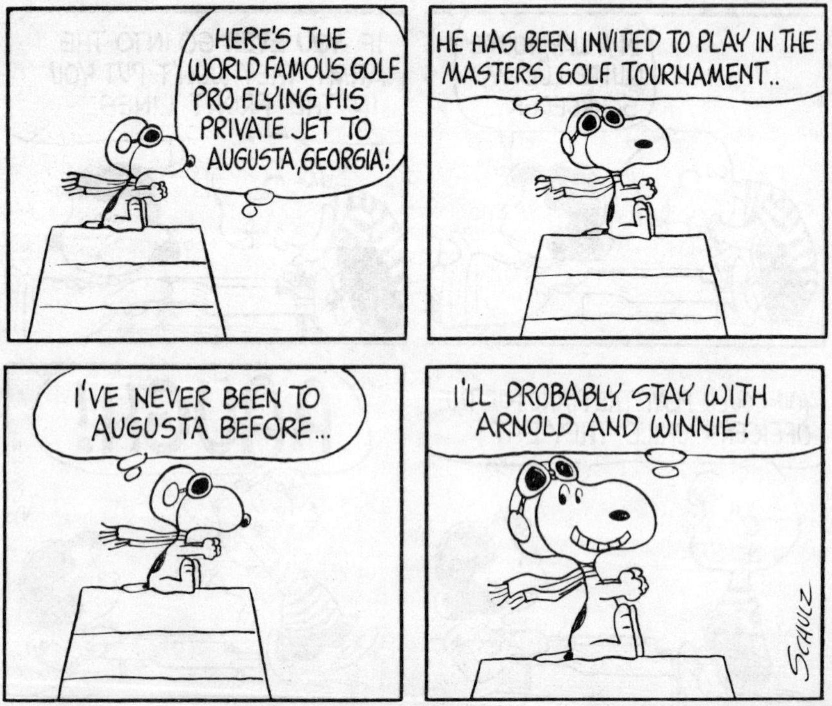
HERE'S THE WORLD FAMOUS GOLF PRO FLYING HIS PRIVATE JET TO AUGUSTA, GEORGIA!
HE HAS BEEN INVITED TO PLAY IN THE MASTERS GOLF TOURNAMENT..
I'VE NEVER BEEN TO AUGUSTA BEFORE...
I'LL PROBABLY STAY WITH ARNOLD AND WINNIE!
SCHULZ

HERE'S THE WORLD FAMOUS GOLF PRO GOING OUT TO PLAY A PRACTICE ROUND AT THE MASTERS
I'LL PROBABLY PLAY WITH ARNIE TODAY, OR SAM, OR BEN, OR GAY...
OF COURSE, THEY DON'T ALWAYS LIKE TO PLAY WITH ME...
THEY HATE IT WHEN I OUTDRIVE THEM!
SCHULZ

HERE'S THE WORLD FAMOUS GOLF PRO TEEING OFF ON THE FIRST HOLE AT THE MASTERS...
AS HE WALKS DOWN THE FIRST FAIRWAY, HE IS FOLLOWED BY THAT HUGE THRONG OF HIS ADMIRERS KNOWN AS "SNOOPY'S SQUAD"
WINTER RULES?
SCHULZ

IT'S THE SECOND DAY OF THE BIG MASTERS GOLF TOURNAMENT IN AUGUSTA, GEORGIA..
NO MOVIE CAMERAS, PLEASE!
HERE'S THE WORLD-FAMOUS GOLF PRO LINING UP HIS PUTT ON THE SIXTEENTH GREEN.........
SCHULZ

WHAT ARE YOU DOING HOME?
I THOUGHT YOU WERE IN AUGUSTA PLAYING IN THE MASTERS GOLF TOURNAMENT..DIDN'T YOU MAKE THE CUT?
HOW COME YOU'RE NOT PLAYING IN THE FINAL ROUND?
WELL, I RAN INTO THIS CUTE LITTLE GEORGIA BEAGLE, SEE...
SCHULZ

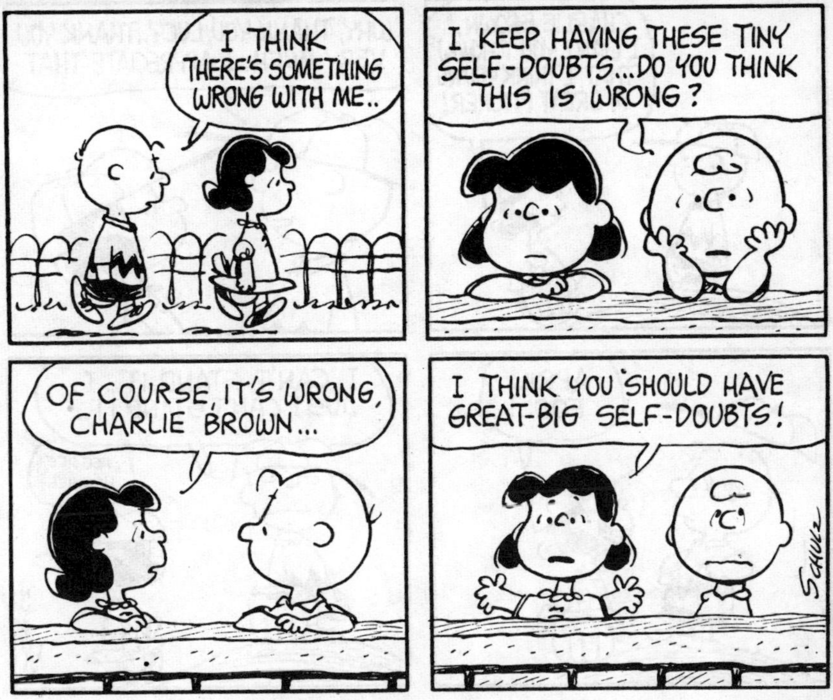
I THINK THERE'S SOMETHING WRONG WITH ME..
I KEEP HAVING THESE TINY SELF-DOUBTS...DO YOU THINK THIS IS WRONG?
OF COURSE, IT'S WRONG, CHARLIE BROWN...
I THINK YOU SHOULD HAVE GREAT-BIG SELF-DOUBTS!
SCHULZ

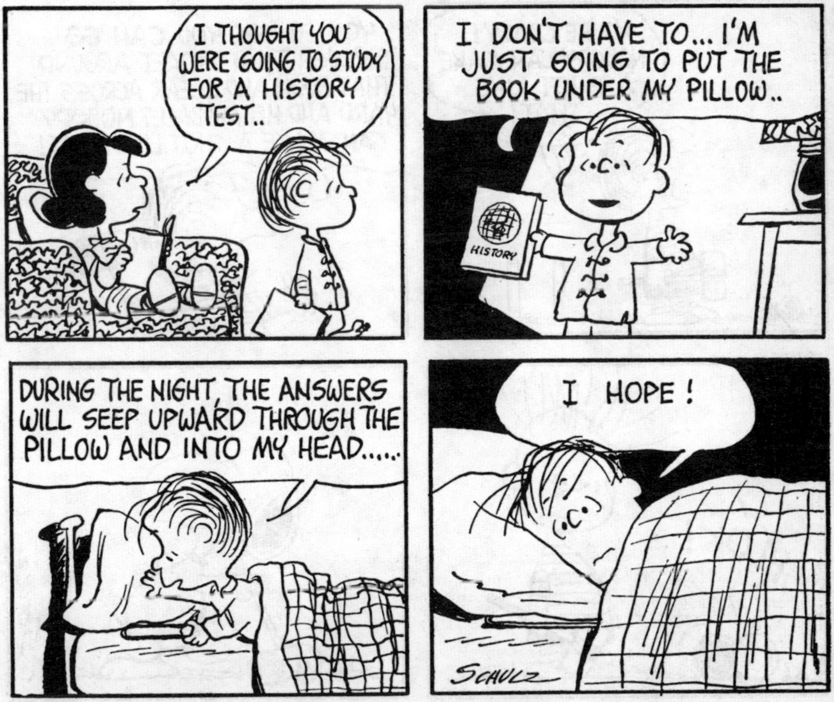
I THOUGHT YOU WERE GOING TO STUDY FOR A HISTORY TEST..
I DON'T HAVE TO... I'M JUST GOING TO PUT THE BOOK UNDER MY PILLOW..
HISTORY
DURING THE NIGHT, THE ANSWERS WILL SEEP UPWARD THROUGH THE PILLOW AND INTO MY HEAD.....
I HOPE!
SCHULZ

CHARLIE BROWN, I WANT YOU TO KNOW THAT I THINK YOU'RE A GREAT PITCHER!
WHY, THANK YOU, LUCY..THANK YOU VERY MUCH..I APPRECIATE THAT
APRIL FOOL!
I CAN'T STAND IT... I JUST CAN'T STAND IT...
HEE HEE HEE HEE
SCHULZ

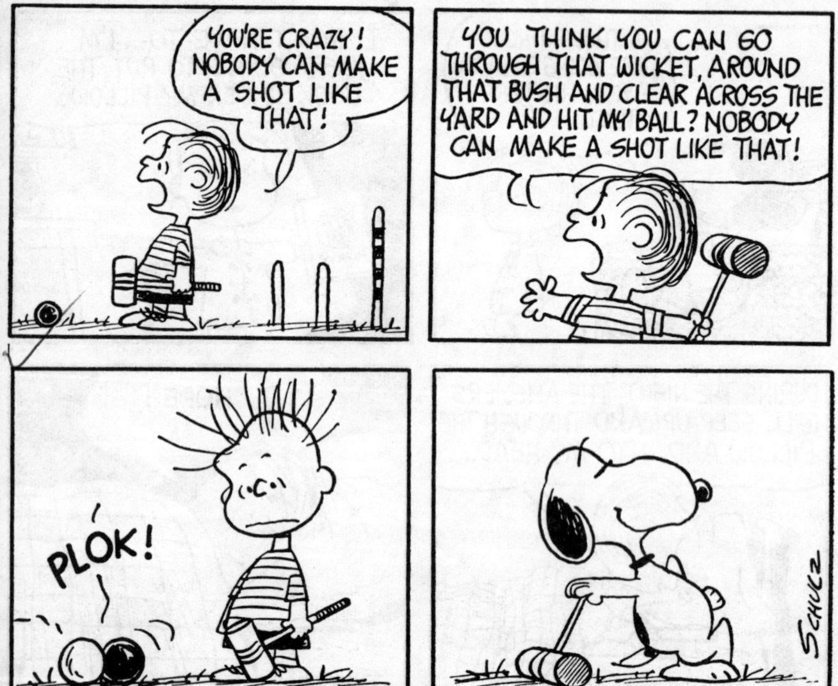
YOU'RE CRAZY! NOBODY CAN MAKE A SHOT LIKE THAT!
YOU THINK YOU CAN GO THROUGH THAT WICKET, AROUND THAT BUSH AND CLEAR ACROSS THE YARD AND HIT MY BALL? NOBODY CAN MAKE A SHOT LIKE THAT!
PLOK!
SCHULZ

THIS IS "BE KIND TO ANIMALS" WEEK
THIS IS "BE KIND TO ANIMALS" WEEK
SCHULZ

I'LL NEVER GET TO THE FIRST GRADE
I'M ALMOST SURE THEY'RE GOING TO MAKE ME GO THROUGH KINDERGARTEN AGAIN
WHY?
I FAILED FLOWER-BRINGING!!
SCHULZ

?
FANTASTIC!
DO YOU REALIZE THAT THEY MAY HAVE TO REPLANT EVERY TREE IN THIS PARK?
I CAN'T STAND IT.. I JUST CAN'T STAND IT...
SCHULZ

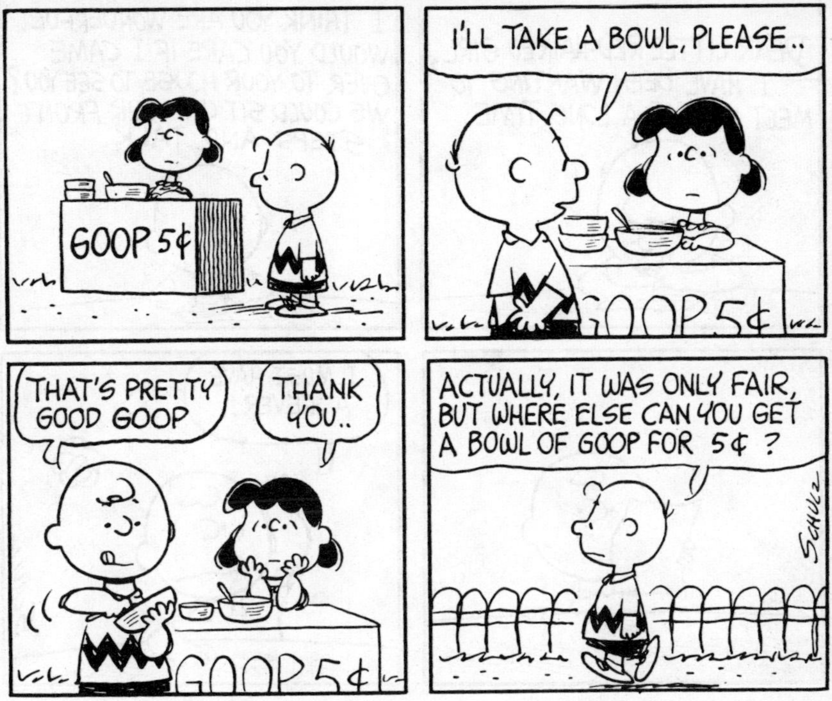
I'LL TAKE A BOWL, PLEASE..
THAT'S PRETTY GOOD GOOP
THANK YOU..
ACTUALLY, IT WAS ONLY FAIR, BUT WHERE ELSE CAN YOU GET A BOWL OF GOOP FOR 5¢ ?
GOOP 5¢
SCHULZ

COME ON, TRY IT... IF YOU DON'T HAVE THE CASH, YOU CAN PUT IT ON YOUR CREDIT CARD...
YOU WOULDN'T KNOW GOOD GOOP IF YOU TASTED IT !!!
GOOP 5¢
SCHULZ

DEAR LITTLE RED-HAIRED GIRL, I HAVE BEEN WANTING TO MEET YOU FOR A LONG TIME.
I THINK YOU ARE WONDERFUL. WOULD YOU CARE IF I CAME OVER TO YOUR HOUSE TO SEE YOU? WE COULD SIT ON YOUR FRONT STEPS AND TALK.
I MUST HAVE A FEVER!
SCHULZ

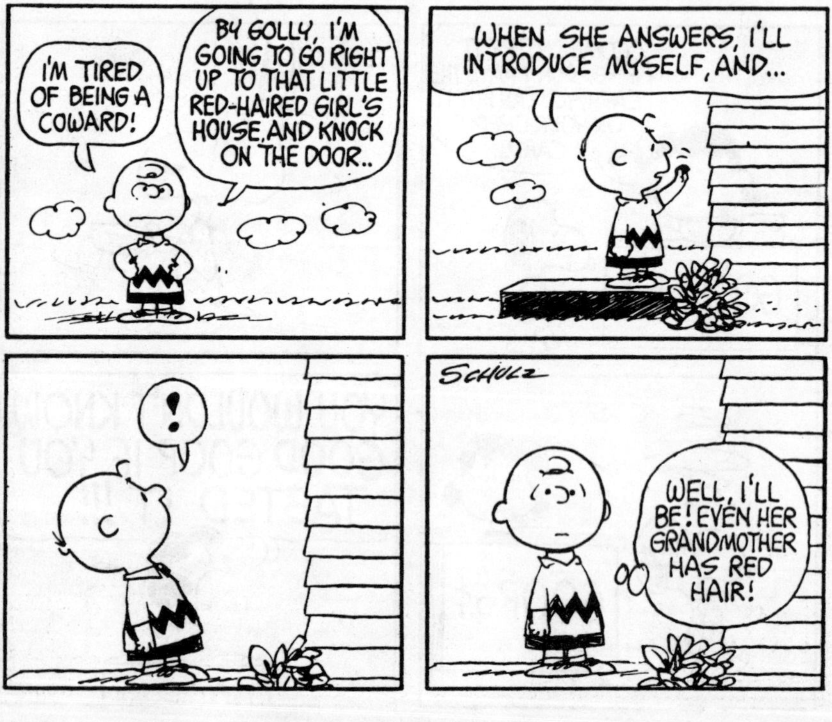
I'M TIRED OF BEING A COWARD!
BY GOLLY, I'M GOING TO GO RIGHT UP TO THAT LITTLE RED-HAIRED GIRL'S HOUSE, AND KNOCK ON THE DOOR..
WHEN SHE ANSWERS, I'LL INTRODUCE MYSELF, AND...
!
SCHULZ
WELL, I'LL BE! EVEN HER GRANDMOTHER HAS RED HAIR!

HELLO...I...UH..
I...I...I..UH..
I...I....UH..I JUST...UH...
I..I...I.....I.......I.....
YOU'RE A CUTE GRANDMOTHER!
OH, BROTHER!!
SCHULZ

I'LL NEVER GET TO MEET THAT LITTLE RED-HAIRED GIRL...
SOMETIMES I GET SO DEPRESSED I CAN HARDLY STAND IT..
ONE BOWL, PLEASE..
GOOP 5¢
A GOOD WAY TO FORGET A LOVE AFFAIR IS TO EAT A LOT OF GOOP!
SCHULZ

PSYCHIAT
HELP
OKAY, WHAT'S YOUR PROBLEM?
THE DOCTOR
PSYCHIATRIC HELP 5¢
TOMORROW!
THE DOCTOR IS IN
PSYCHIATRIC HELP 5¢
I FIND MYSELF ALWAYS WORRYING ABOUT TOMORROW..
THE DOCTOR IS IN
THEN WHEN TOMORROW BECOMES TODAY, I START WORRYING ABOUT TOMORROW AGAIN..
I GUESS I'M JUST AFRAID TO FACE THE FUTURE
I THINK I CAN HELP YOU, CHARLIE BROWN...
THE DOCTOR IS IN
NOW, THE FIRST THING YOU HAVE TO DO IS TURN AROUND...
THE FUTURE IS OVER THIS WAY... THERE, THAT'S BETTER!
!
NOW, THE NEXT THING IS YOUR POSTURE... IF YOU'RE GOING TO FACE THE FUTURE, YOU'VE GOT TO DO IT WITH YOUR CHEST OUT..
THAT'S THE WAY! THROW OUT YOUR CHEST AND FACE THE FUTURE! NOW, RAISE YOUR ARM AND CLENCH YOUR FIST..THAT'S RIGHT.. NOW, LOOK DETERMINED...
WELL, I THINK I KNOW WHY YOU'RE AFRAID TO FACE THE FUTURE..
WHY?
YOU LOOK RIDICULOUS!
SCHULZ

HAPPY FATHER'S DAY from your rare gem.
HI, ROY... I SUPPOSE YOU'RE WONDERING WHAT I'M DOING...
I'VE JUST MADE MY DAD A HAND-MADE FATHER'S DAY CARD..
EVERY NOW AND THEN MY DAD SAYS TO ME, "PEPPERMINT PATTY, DO YOU KNOW WHAT YOU ARE?" AND I ALWAYS SAY, "NO"....THEN HE SAYS TO ME, "YOU ARE A RARE GEM!" AND WE BOTH LAUGH...
SO YOU SEE, I'VE MADE A CARD FOR HIM... "HAPPY FATHER'S DAY FROM YOUR RARE GEM"
THAT'S VERY NICE..
THANK YOU..I'LL PUT IT ON TOP OF HIS DRESSER WHERE HE'LL SEE IT...
ACTUALLY, ANYONE WHO GIVES HIS DAD A FATHER'S DAY CARD IS A RARE GEM...
SCHULZ

SCHROEDER, WHAT WOULD HAPPEN IF YOU AND I GOT MARRIED SOMEDAY, AND I GOT TIRED OF FIXING YOUR BREAKFAST?
I MEAN, WHAT WOULD HAPPEN IF I DECIDED I'D RATHER SLEEP IN THE MORNING?
I CAN'T STAND IT...
SAY, FOR INSTANCE, I GOT TIRED OF GETTING UP EVERY MORNING TO FIX YOUR BREAKFAST, AND JUST SUDDENLY DECIDED I'D RATHER SLEEP LATE EVERY MORNING...
I MEAN, WHAT WOULD YOUR REACTION BE?
ROWRR!!
WELL, PERHAPS I COULD SLEEP LATE ON WEEKENDS...
SCHULZ

WATCH IT, BEAGLE!
SIGH
SCHULZ

YOU SPEND ALL YOUR TIME LYING ON TOP OF THAT DOG HOUSE..
THAT'S ALL YOU SEEM TO DO... YOU JUST LIE THERE AND LIE THERE
I JUST DON'T SEE HOW YOU DO IT!
LET'S NOT OVERLOOK THE POSSIBILITY OF GENIUS!
SCHULZ

I HAVE A MESSAGE FOR YOU...
MOM SAYS GET YOUR STUPID SELF IN THERE, AND CLEAN UP YOUR STUPID ROOM!
I'M SURE SHE DIDN'T SAY IT QUITE LIKE THAT
SO I ELABORATED A LITTLE..
SCHULZ

I WISH SHE'D MISS...
MISS! MISS! MISS! MISS!
THIS IS THE MOST BORING THING I'VE EVER DONE... I CAN'T STAND HERE ALL DAY TURNING THIS STUPID ROPE... WHY DOESN'T SHE EVER MISS?
THIS COULD GO ON FOREVER.. I'VE GOT TO GET HOME.. I HAVE A WHOLE LOT OF HOMEWORK TO DO, AND MY FAVORITE TV PROGRAM COMES ON IN FIFTEEN MINUTES AND, BESIDES, MY ARM IS KILLING ME!
IF SHE'D JUST MISS, MAYBE I'D HAVE AN OPENING TO SUGGEST THAT WE QUIT.. WHY DOESN'T SHE EVER MISS? MISS! MISS! MISS! RATS! SHE NEVER MISSES! WHY DON'T I JUST TELL HER I'M GOING HOME?
THAT'S WHAT I THINK I'LL DO... I THINK I'LL JUST TELL HER THAT I HAVE TO QUIT AND GO HOME... I THINK I'LL JUST DROP THE ROPE, AND TELL HER I'M GOING HOME.... MISS! MISS! MISS!
MY ARM IS GETTING NUMB... I CAN'T EVEN FEEL MY FINGERS ANY MORE.. I THINK I'LL JUST THROW THE ROPE DOWN, AND TELL HER I'M QUITTING... I THINK I'LL JUST LET GO, AND WALK AWAY... I..
TEN THOUSAND! TEN THOUSAND AND ONE, TEN THOUSAND AND TWO..
SIGH!
SCHULZ

HAVE YOU SEEN OUR BASEBALL SCHEDULE FOR THIS YEAR, "CHUCK"?
MY TEAM PLAYS YOUR TEAM TWELVE TIMES...WE SLAUGHTER YOU TWICE IN APRIL, SMASH YOU THREE TIMES IN MAY AND RUIN YOU ONCE IN JUNE..
WE MURDER YOU TWICE IN JULY, ANNIHILATE YOU THREE TIMES IN AUGUST AND POUND YOU ONCE IN SEPTEMBER
IT'S A GREAT SCHEDULE, HUH, "CHUCK"?
BEAUTIFUL!
SCHULZ

THIS YEAR WE'RE GOING TO STRESS PROPER CONDITIONING..
I WANT EACH PLAYER TO DO TWENTY PUSHUPS EVERY DAY!
HOW ABOUT ONE PUSHUP EVERY TWENTY DAYS?
WHAT A CRABBY MANAGER..
SCHULZ

HEY, MANAGER, I CAN'T DO TWENTY PUSHUPS...
WELL, MAYBE YOU SHOULD START WITH JUST FIFTEEN OR MAYBE TEN...LET ME DEMONSTRATE...
PUSHUPS CAN BE VERY DIFFICULT IF YOU'RE OUT OF SHAPE..SOMETIMES IT'S BEST TO START WITH JUST...
...ONE !
SCHULZ

IT'S GETTING DARK..I GUESS THAT'S ENOUGH PRACTICE FOR TODAY..
YOU THINK I DON'T CARE ABOUT OUR TEAM, DON'T YOU, CHARLIE BROWN?
WELL, JUST TO SHOW YOU THAT I DO, I'VE FIGURED OUT A WAY FOR US TO PLAY NIGHT GAMES!
GO AHEAD... GO OUT ON THE PITCHER'S MOUND, AND SEE..

THERE'S ANOTHER GOOD THING ABOUT PLAYING NIGHT GAMES, CHARLIE BROWN..
SAY YOU'RE PITCHING A LOUSY GAME, SEE, AND WE WANT TO GET YOU OUT OF THERE...WELL, ALL WE HAVE TO DO IS COME OUT TO THE MOUND AND BLOW OUT YOUR CANDLE!
POOF!
I THINK WE'D BETTER STICK TO DAY GAMES!
SCHULZ

I WAS WATCHING THIS BALL GAME ON TV LAST YEAR..
ONE OF THE PLAYERS GOT REAL MAD AT THE UMPIRE, AND KICKED DIRT ON HIM...
...LIKE THIS!
YOU CAN LEARN A LOT WATCHING THOSE GAMES ON TV!
SCHULZ

NOW, LOOK HERE.. I DON'T THINK YOU'RE EVEN TRYING!
BLEAH!
COME BACK HERE!! YOU CAN'T QUIT THE TEAM BEFORE THE SEASON EVEN STARTS!
I SHOULDN'T HAVE ACCUSED HIM OF NOT TRYING...BEAGLE-SHORTSTOPS ARE SO SENSITIVE...
SCHULZ

WHAT'LL WE DO? SNOOPY'S QUIT THE TEAM!
ALL I DID WAS BAWL HIM OUT A LITTLE..
DON'T BLAME YOURSELF, CHARLIE BROWN...
THAT'S THE TROUBLE WITH THAT STUPID DOG...HE'S ALWAYS CHANGING RAINBOWS!
"CHANGING RAINBOWS"?!
SCHULZ

PLEASE COME BACK TO THE TEAM, SNOOPY...
IF YOU COME BACK, I'LL DO ANYTHING! I'LL RAISE YOUR FOOD ALLOWANCE... YOU CAN PLAY ANY POSITION YOU WANT.. YOU CAN EVEN BE MANAGER!
MANAGER?
HERE'S THE WORLD FAMOUS BASEBALL MANAGER STANDING IN THE DUGOUT..
NOW WHAT HAVE I DONE?
SCHULZ

MANAGER?
THAT STUPID BEAGLE IS GOING TO BE OUR NEW MANAGER? NOTHING DOING! I'LL..
BOOT!
WE BASEBALL MANAGERS DON'T STAND FOR ANY BACK-TALK!
SCHULZ

STRIKE THREE!
BOOT!
THIS NEW MANAGER IS GOING TO BE ROUGH TO PLAY FOR!
SCHULZ

KLUNK!
BOOT!
BOOT!
SCHULZ

IT'S KIND OF NICE NOT BEING MANAGER..
ON THE NIGHT BEFORE OUR GAMES I ALWAYS USED TO LIE AWAKE WORRYING...
I WONDER IF OUR NEW MANAGER IS LYING AWAKE WORRYING...
Z
SCHULZ

HERE WE GO... THE FIRST PITCH OF THE SEASON!
GOOD GRIEF! A HOME RUN!!
BOOT!
SCHULZ

OH, OH! OUR NEW MANAGER IS GIVING ME THE SIGNAL TO STEAL SECOND..
"YOU'RE OUT!!"
BOOT!
SCHULZ

WELL, WE LOST OUR FIRST GAME OF THE SEASON..
I WONDER HOW OUR NEW MANAGER WILL TAKE THIS DEFEAT?
BOOT! BOOT! BOOT!
BOOT!
BOOT! BOOT! BOOT!
I HATE LOSING!
SCHULZ

CHARLIE BROWN, WHEN A TEAM LOSES A GAME, IS IT THE FAULT OF THE PLAYERS OR THE MANAGER?
WELL, I DON'T KNOW...IT'S KIND OF HARD TO SAY, AND I...
WELL, I'M NOT AFRAID TO SAY! WHEN A TEAM LOSES A GAME, I THINK IT'S THE FAULT OF THE MANAGER!
BOOT!
SCHULZ

ACTUALLY, RUNNING A BALL CLUB IS A VERY HARD JOB
IF YOU WANT, I'LL BE GLAD TO TAKE OVER AS MANAGER AGAIN.....
SMAK!
A KISS ON THE NOSE, AND I'M OFF THE HOOK!
SCHULZ

IF I HAVE A BIRTHDAY PARTY, WILL YOU GIRLS COME?
WELL, FRANKLY, CHARLIE BROWN, WE'D RATHER NOT...
BUT IF WE CAN'T FIND ANYTHING ELSE TO DO, AND IF THERE'S NOTHING GOOD ON TV THAT DAY, WE MIGHT CONSIDER COMING...
IT'S FUN TO GIVE A PARTY WHEN EVERYONE'S SO ENTHUSIASTIC
SCHULZ

BEEP!
I HAVEN'T BEEPED YOU IN A LONG TIME
I HAVEN'T MISSED IT A BIT!
SCHULZ

DANGER! Kite-eating tree
HELLO, YOU DIRTY KITE-EATING TREE! HAVE YOU HAD A HARD WINTER? I'LL BET YOU'RE HUNGRY, AREN'T YOU?
I'LL ALSO BET THAT YOU HATE ME, DON'T YOU? YOU HATE ME BECAUSE I RECOGNIZE YOU FOR WHAT YOU ARE, A DIRTY, SCHEMING, NO-GOOD, KITE-EATING TREE!
YOU ALSO HATE ME BECAUSE YOU NEED ME! I'M THE ONLY ONE AROUND HERE WHO FLIES KITES, AND WITHOUT ME, YOU'D GET PRETTY HUNGRY!
WHAT WOULD YOU DO IF I DECIDED NOT TO FLY ANY KITES THIS YEAR? WHAT WOULD YOU DO?
YOU'D STARVE TO DEATH, THAT'S WHAT YOU'D DO!
IT SORT OF SHAKES YOU UP, DOESN'T IT? WITHOUT ME, YOU'RE NOTHING!!
EXCUSE ME, CHARLIE BROWN, BUT YOU LOOK SORT OF DIFFERENT... LIKE SOME CHANGE HAS COME OVER YOU...
I THINK MAYBE IT HAS...
FOR THE FIRST TIME IN MY LIFE I FEEL NEEDED!
SCHULZ

POW!
YOU HAVE CUTE TOES, CHARLIE BROWN!
SCHULZ

THIS IS THE SAME THING I HAD TO EAT YESTERDAY..
IN FACT, THIS IS THE SAME THING I HAD TO EAT EVERY DAY FOR THE PAST MONTH!
I THINK I'LL REGISTER A COMPLAINT...
AFTER I'VE FINISHED EATING!
SCHULZ

DO YOU KNOW HOW MANY STARS THERE ARE IN THE SKY, LUCY?
OF COURSE! THREE HUNDRED AND SIXTY-FIVE... ONE FOR EACH DAY IN THE YEAR..
WE LIVE IN WHAT IS KNOWN AS AN ORDERLY UNIVERSE!
SCHULZ

LUCY SAYS THERE ARE THREE HUNDRED AND SIXTY-FIVE STARS IN THE SKY..
SHE SAYS THERE'S ONE FOR EACH DAY IN THE YEAR...
SO MUCH FOR TODAY!
SCHULZ

SOMEDAY, I'D LIKE TO PUNCH A CAT IN THE NOSE!
I WONDER IF I'D EVER HAVE THE NERVE TO TRY IT...
PROBABLY NOT
IT'S KIND OF FUN TO THINK ABOUT, THOUGH..
SCHULZ

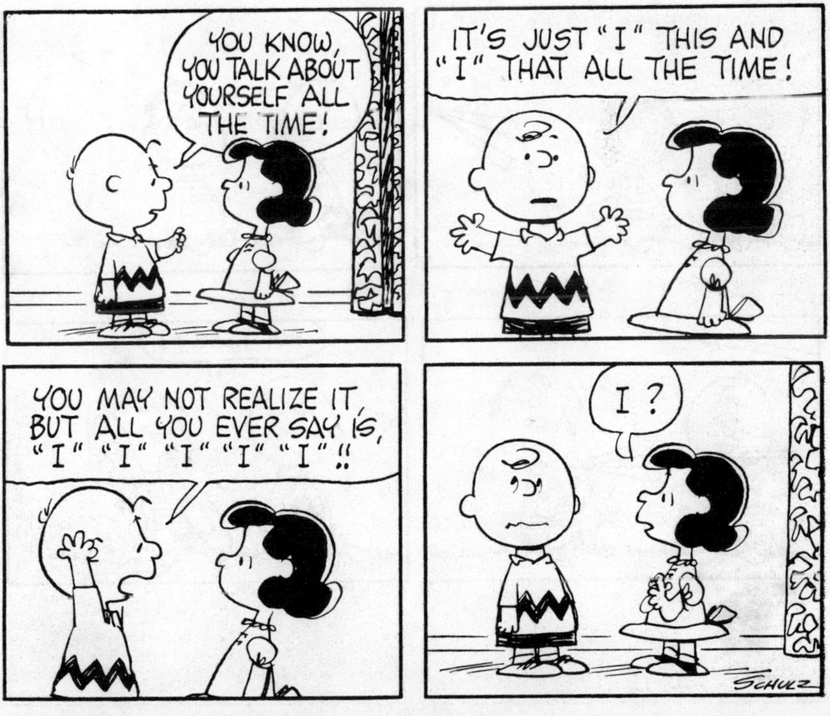
YOU KNOW, YOU TALK ABOUT YOURSELF ALL THE TIME!
IT'S JUST "I" THIS AND "I" THAT ALL THE TIME!
YOU MAY NOT REALIZE IT, BUT ALL YOU EVER SAY IS, "I" "I" "I" "I" "I"!!
I?
SCHULZ

DON'T YOU EVER GET TIRED OF THAT BLANKET ?
NOT REALLY !
SCHULZ

KLUNK!
KLUNK!
YOU CAN'T DO ANYTHING, CAN YOU, CHARLIE BROWN?
SCHULZ

WELL, SO LONG, ROY... I'M OFF TO CAMP!
THIS YEAR I'M IN CHARGE OF A TENT... I'M ALMOST LIKE A COUNSELOR...ISN'T THAT GREAT?
I LOVE GOING TO CAMP..
FOR A GIRL LIKE ME, IT'S THE NEXT BEST THING TO BEING IN THE INFANTRY!
SCHULZ

HELLO, GIRLS... I'M "PEPPERMINT" PATTY, YOUR TENT MONITOR...
ACTUALLY, MY NAME REALLY ISN'T "PEPPERMINT" PATTY...THAT'S JUST A NICK-NAME MY DAD GAVE ME... HE ALSO CALLS ME HIS "RARE GEM"
NOW, WHAT ARE YOUR NAMES?
AFTER ALL THAT, WHAT CAN WE SAY?
SCHULZ

"SOPHIE, CLARA AND SHIRLEY.."
NOW, LET'S SEE IF I HAVE YOU STRAIGHT..A GOOD TENT MONITOR MUST KNOW THE NAMES OF ALL THE GIRLS IN HER TENT..
YOU'RE SOPHIE, YOU'RE CLARA AND YOU'RE SHIRLEY.... RIGHT?
WRONG!
BUT THAT'S CLOSE ENOUGH.. WE'RE ONLY GONNA BE HERE FOR TWO WEEKS...
SCHULZ

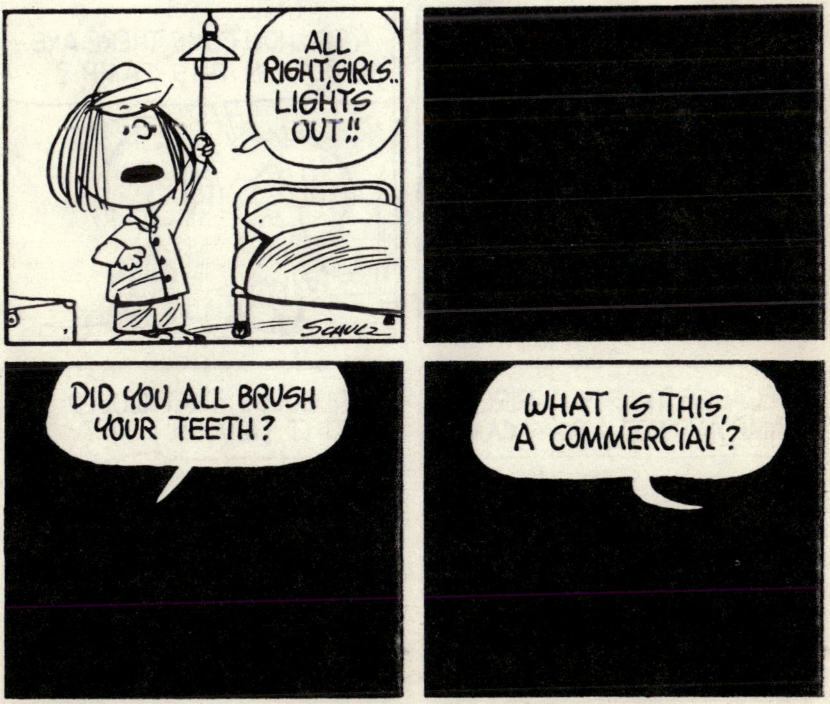
ALL RIGHT, GIRLS.. LIGHTS OUT!!
SCHULZ
DID YOU ALL BRUSH YOUR TEETH?
WHAT IS THIS, A COMMERCIAL?

ALL RIGHT, GIRLS..THIS IS YOUR SWIMMING TEST...
YOU ARE TO SWIM BACK AND FORTH ACROSS THE POOL SIX TIMES "FREE STYLE"
THEN YOU ARE TO SWIM BACK AND FORTH TWICE USING THE BACKSTROKE AND BACK AND FORTH TWICE USING THE BUTTERFLY STROKE..ANY QUESTIONS?
IS THIS WITH OR WITHOUT LIFE-JACKETS ?

YOU HAVE A QUESTION, SOPHIE?
YES...HOW COME THERE ARE NO BOYS IN THIS CAMP ?
BECAUSE THIS IS A GIRLS' CAMP AND NOT A BOYS' CAMP
I GUESS THAT WOULD DO IT, WOULDN'T IT ?

June 24
Dear Dad,
How are you?
I am fine.
This is my second week at camp and we are having a good time.
I have three little girls in my tent. I am the tent monitor. I have been teaching them all about camping.
I'll be home soon.
Love,
Peppermint Patty
(your rare gem)
SCHULZ

TRAMPOLINE!
I KNOW
SCHULZ

SIR, I'M LONESOME, AND I WANT TO GO HOME..
LONESOME?! HOW CAN YOU BE LONESOME IN A PLACE SO FULL OF KIDS? HOW CAN YOU BE LONESOME WHEN THERE'S SO MUCH TO DO AROUND HERE?
SOPHIE, HOW CAN YOU POSSIBLY BE LONESOME IN A PLACE LIKE THIS?
THE MORE YOU TALK, THE MORE LONESOME I GET!
CAMP KAMP
SCHULZ

SOPHIE, WE'VE GOT TO CURE YOUR LONESOMENESS..
CAMP KAMP
WHY DON'T WE WRITE A LETTER TO YOUR FOLKS? JUST TALKING WITH THEM AND TELLING THEM ALL ABOUT WHAT YOU'VE BEEN DOING WILL GET YOUR MIND OFF YOUR PROBLEMS...
YOU DICTATE WHAT YOU WANT TO SAY, AND I'LL WRITE IT..
DEAR MOM AND DAD, I'M LONESOME..
THAT ISN'T EXACTLY WHAT I MEANT!
SCHULZ

SOPHIE, YOU'RE SMILING!
I'M NOT LONESOME ANY MORE.. I MET THIS KEEN LITTLE KID FROM THE BOYS' CAMP ACROSS THE LAKE...HE'S MY FRIEND!
WAIT HERE...I'LL BRING HIM TO YOU...
SCHULZ

WELL, CLARA, IT'S BEEN A PRETTY GOOD TWO WEEKS, HASN'T IT?
I'M GOING TO MISS YOU GIRLS.. WHERE'S SOPHIE?
SHE'S OVER THERE SAYING GOOD-BY TO HER FRIEND..
CAMP KAMP
SNIF
SNIF
I DON'T KNOW..I LIKE HIM AND HE'S A GOOD SHORTSTOP AND ALL THAT, BUT I STILL SAY HE'S THE FUNNIEST LOOKING KID I'VE EVER SEEN
SCHULZ

IS THIS YOUR BAT, CHARLIE BROWN? IT DOESN'T HAVE YOUR NAME ON IT...
YOU SHOULD HAVE YOUR NAME ON YOURS LIKE ALL OF THE BIG LEAGUE PLAYERS
LINUS HAS A WOOD-BURNING SET AT HOME... WHY DON'T I TAKE YOUR BAT, AND PUT YOUR NAME ON IT?
SAY! THIS IS GOING TO BE GREAT!
I'LL BE THE ONLY ONE AROUND HERE WITH HIS NAME ON A BAT!
THIS WILL REALLY IMPRESS THE KIDS ON THE OTHER TEAMS WE PLAY...THEY'LL BE AFRAID TO SEE ME STEP UP TO THE PLATE... THEY'LL THINK I'M A BIG-LEAGUER, AND I'LL...
HERE'S YOUR BAT, CHARLIE BROWN!
I HAD A LITTLE TROUBLE WITH THE WOOD-BURNING SET...
SCHULZ

DID YOU SEE HOW I STRUCK OUT THAT LAST KID? PRETTY GOOD PITCHING, HUH?
YEAH, THAT WAS THAT KID WHO'S BEEN SICK IN BED ALL WINTER..HIS DOCTOR SAYS HE'S GOING TO BE ALL RIGHT, BUT TO GET OUT IN THE SUN...
HE ALSO DOESN'T SEE VERY WELL, AND HE'S NEVER PLAYED BASEBALL BEFORE...
SOMETIMES A CATCHER CAN KNOW TOO MUCH ABOUT THE OPPOSITION...
SCHULZ

POW!
..AND WE FOUND YOUR CAP OVER TWO BLOCKS AWAY, AND ONE OF YOUR SHOES THREE BLOCKS AWAY, AND ONE OF YOUR SOCKS TWO BLOCKS AWAY, AND..
ALL RIGHT!
SCHULZ

CRACK!
CLOMP!
IN APPRECIATION OF THE GREAT PLAY YOU MADE THIS AFTERNOON, SNOOPY, THE TEAM HAS ASKED ME TO PRESENT YOU THIS...
HOW NICE... THE "GOLDEN MOUTH" AWARD!
SCHULZ

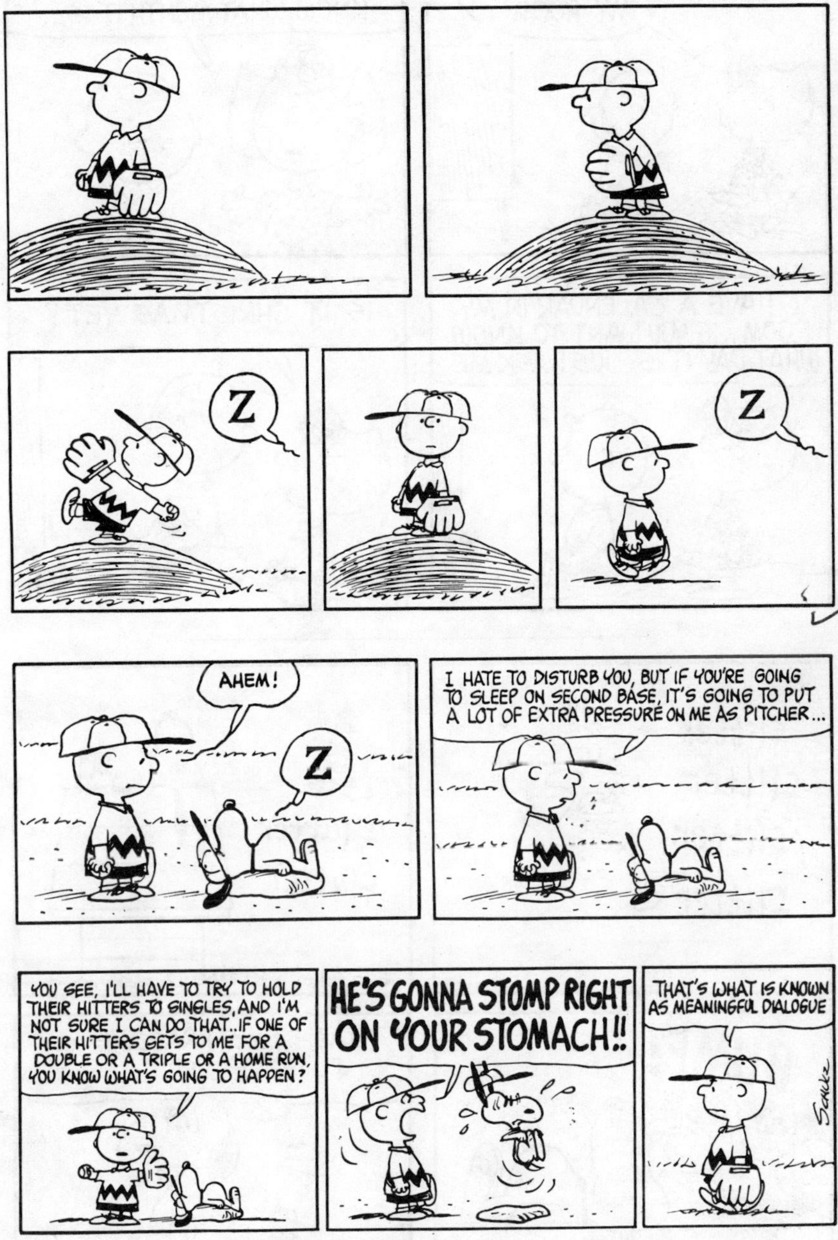
Z
Z
AHEM!
Z
I HATE TO DISTURB YOU, BUT IF YOU'RE GOING TO SLEEP ON SECOND BASE, IT'S GOING TO PUT A LOT OF EXTRA PRESSURE ON ME AS PITCHER...
YOU SEE, I'LL HAVE TO TRY TO HOLD THEIR HITTERS TO SINGLES, AND I'M NOT SURE I CAN DO THAT..IF ONE OF THEIR HITTERS GETS TO ME FOR A DOUBLE OR A TRIPLE OR A HOME RUN, YOU KNOW WHAT'S GOING TO HAPPEN?
HE'S GONNA STOMP RIGHT ON YOUR STOMACH!!
THAT'S WHAT IS KNOWN AS MEANINGFUL DIALOGUE
SCHULZ

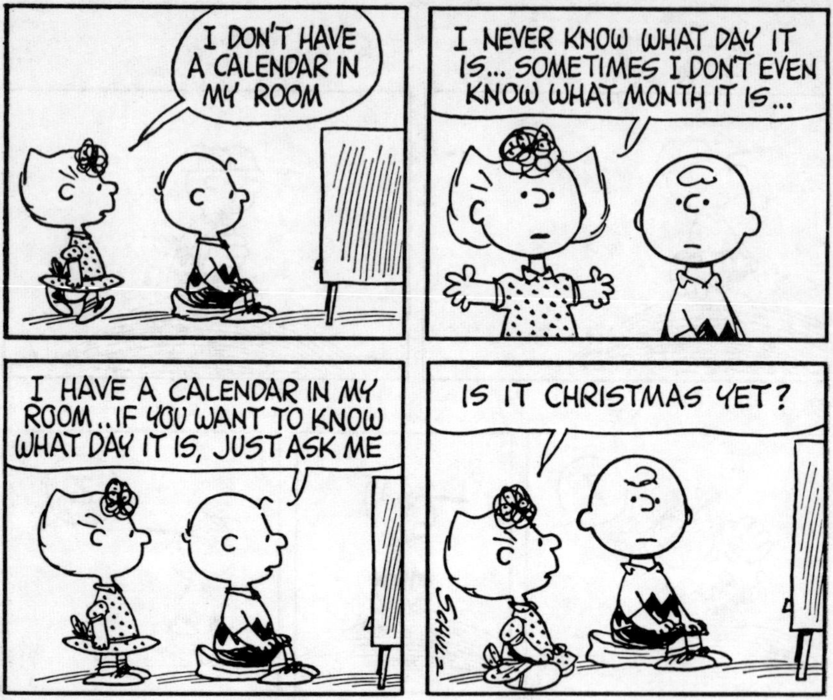
I DON'T HAVE A CALENDAR IN MY ROOM
I NEVER KNOW WHAT DAY IT IS... SOMETIMES I DON'T EVEN KNOW WHAT MONTH IT IS...
I HAVE A CALENDAR IN MY ROOM..IF YOU WANT TO KNOW WHAT DAY IT IS, JUST ASK ME
IS IT CHRISTMAS YET?
SCHULZ

flitter
flitter
flitter
flitter
flutter
flutter
BUMP!
THAT'S EMBARRASSING FOR BOTH OF US...
SCHULZ

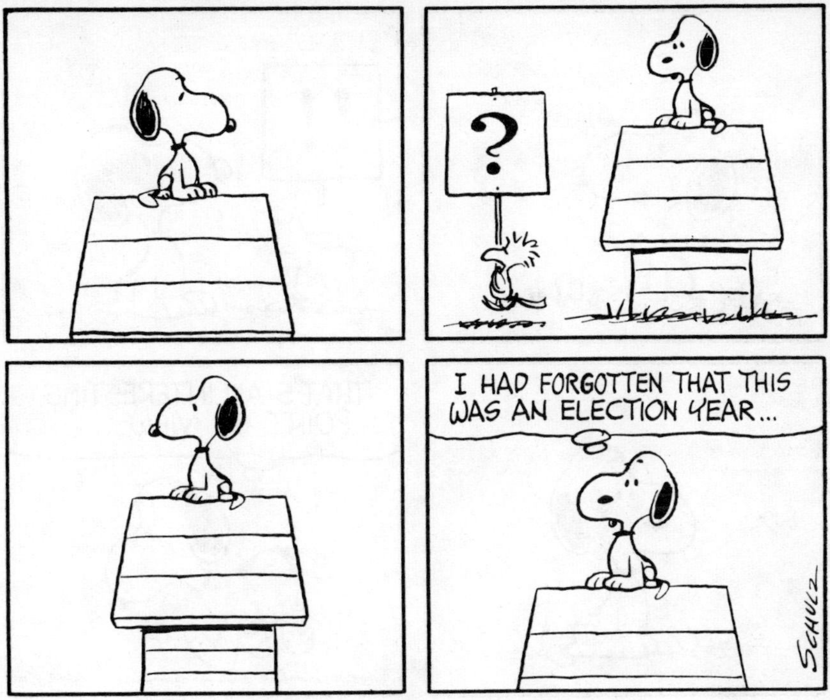
I HAD FORGOTTEN THAT THIS WAS AN ELECTION YEAR...
SCHULZ

HE'S A NICE GUY, BUT I DON'T KNOW WHERE HE STANDS...
SCHULZ

!!
THAT'S AN INTERESTING POINT OF VIEW...
SCHULZ

$
THE ECONOMY CANDIDATE!
¢
SCHULZ

IT LOOKS LIKE A WIDE-OPEN CONVENTION!
SCHULZ

AH!
I KNEW WE'D GET AROUND TO MY KIND OF CANDIDATE...
SCHULZ

LOST AGAIN!
SIGH
WHAT A TEAM...
WE CAN'T EVEN WIN ENOUGH GAMES TO HAVE A SLUMP!
SCHULZ

POW!
HERE'S YOUR CAP, CHARLIE BROWN...
SIGH
SCHULZ

THAT FIRST GUY GOT A HIT, CHARLIE BROWN, BUT DON'T LET IT BOTHER YOU..
I'M UPSIDE DOWN
JUST KEEP THROWIN' 'EM IN THERE!
I'M UPSIDE DOWN
I'M UPSIDE DOWN
SCHULZ

HEY, MANAGER..
I'M UPSIDE DOWN
FRIEDA'S HAVING A PARTY AFTER THE GAME TODAY..
SHE SAYS YOU'RE WELCOME TO COME IF YOU WANT TO
I'M UPSIDE DOWN
SCHULZ

SCHULZ

SCHULZ

HOW SHALL WE PITCH THIS NEXT GUY, CHARLIE BROWN?
WELL, I DON'T KNOW..
THROW HIM YOUR CURVE, CHARLIE BROWN
SAY, HAVE YOU NOTICED HOW BUILT-UP IT'S GETTING AROUND HERE? PRETTY SOON THERE WON'T BE ANY PLACE FOR US TO PLAY.. LOOK AT ALL THE HOUSES...
MY GRAMPA SAYS THAT ALL OF THIS USED TO BE A BIG PASTURE..
HE SAYS HE CAN REMEMBER WHEN THEY USED TO DRIVE CATTLE RIGHT ACROSS HERE
MY DAD SAYS HE COULD HAVE MADE A LOT OF MONEY IF HE HAD BOUGHT THIS LAND TWENTY YEARS AGO
TWENTY YEARS AGO? FIVE YEARS AGO WOULD HAVE BEEN ENOUGH!
THAT'S WHAT I SAY!
OF COURSE! LAND VALUES ARE GOING UP EVERYWHERE
LOOK AT THAT PLACE WHERE THEY PUT UP THE NEW SUPER-MARKET..
THAT'S WHAT MY GRAMPA WAS TALKING ABOUT.. HE SAID YOU COULD HAVE BOUGHT THAT PROPERTY FOR ALMOST NOTHING ONLY TWO YEARS AGO!
WHAT DO YOU THINK, CHARLIE BROWN?
FRANKLY, I THINK HE'D HIT A CURVE BALL...
SCHULZ

I THINK I'VE MADE A NEW THEOLOGICAL DISCOVERY...
WHAT IS IT?
IF YOU HOLD YOUR HANDS UPSIDE DOWN, YOU GET THE OPPOSITE OF WHAT YOU PRAY FOR!
SCHULZ

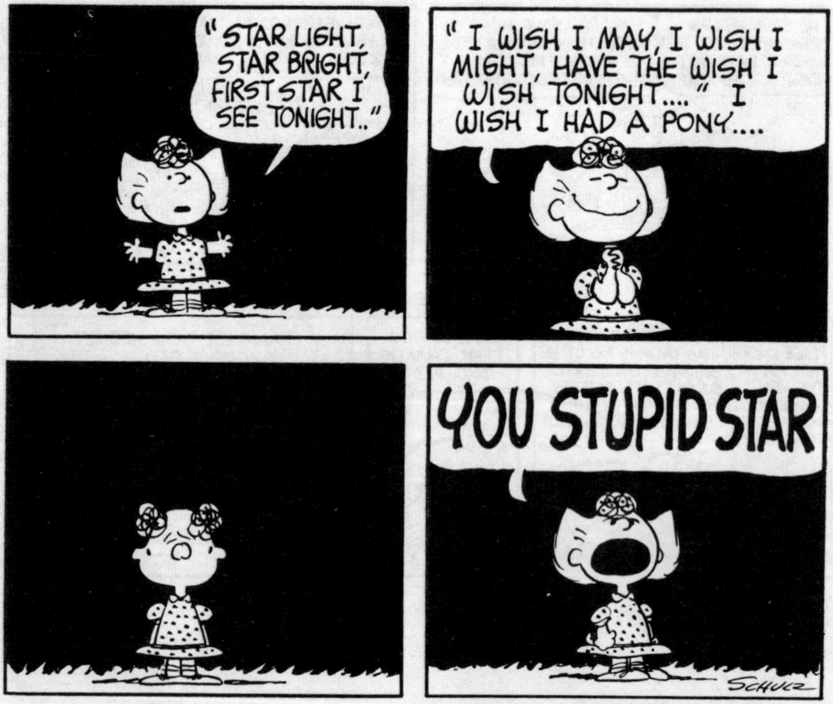
"STAR LIGHT, STAR BRIGHT, FIRST STAR I SEE TONIGHT.."
"I WISH I MAY, I WISH I MIGHT, HAVE THE WISH I WISH TONIGHT...." I WISH I HAD A PONY....
YOU STUPID STAR
SCHULZ

ALL SET, CHARLIE BROWN?
ALL SET!
CATCH A GOOD GAME, DEAR-HEART!
" DEAR-HEART" ?!
SCHULZ

DON'T GIVE UP, CHARLIE BROWN...
WE CAN TAKE THESE GUYS... JUST BEAR DOWN, AND THROW AS HARD AS YOU CAN! WE CAN WIN IF WE REALLY TRY!
THAT'S THE SPIRIT, "DEAR HEART"!
SCHULZ

READY TO START, CHARLIE BROWN?
ALL SET... MY ARM FEELS GREAT!
SHE'S GETTING READY TO SAY IT AGAIN... I CAN JUST FEEL IT...
IF SHE SAYS IT AGAIN, I'LL SCREAM... I KNOW SHE'S JUST WAITING TO SAY IT... SHE..
CATCH A GOOD GAME, "DEAR HEART"!
AAUGH
SCHULZ

CHARLIE BROWN, IF LUCY CALLS ME "DEAR HEART" ONCE MORE, I'M GOING TO QUIT THE TEAM!
ALL RIGHT, TAKE IT EASY... I'LL GO OUT AND TALK TO HER..
WELL, HELLO! DID YOU LEAVE YOUR PITCHER'S MOUND AND COME CLEAR OUT HERE TO CENTER FIELD JUST TO TALK TO **ME**?
I DIDN'T KNOW THE OFFICERS MINGLED WITH THE ENLISTED MEN!
SCHULZ

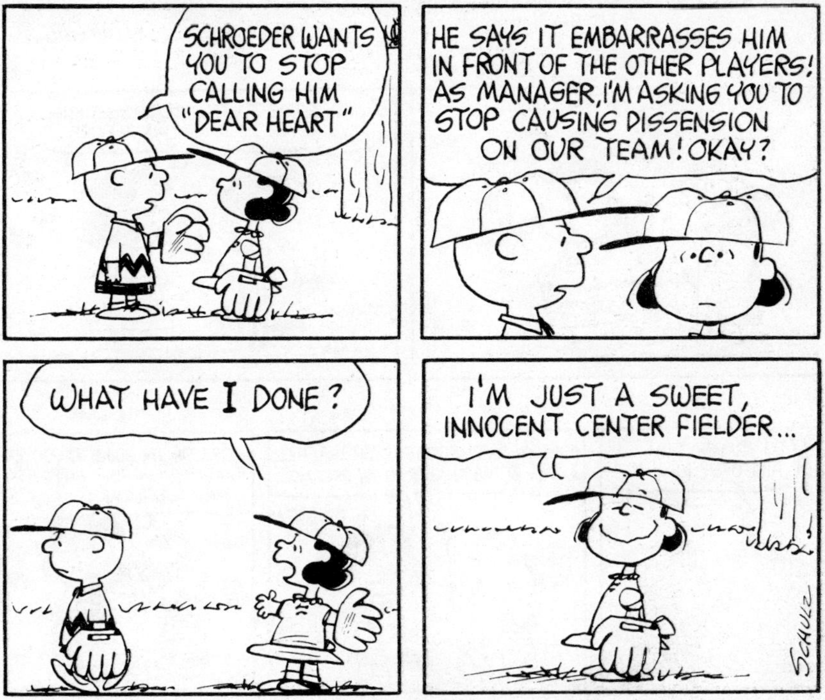
SCHROEDER WANTS YOU TO STOP CALLING HIM "DEAR HEART"
HE SAYS IT EMBARRASSES HIM IN FRONT OF THE OTHER PLAYERS! AS MANAGER, I'M ASKING YOU TO STOP CAUSING DISSENSION ON OUR TEAM! OKAY?
WHAT HAVE I DONE?
I'M JUST A SWEET, INNOCENT CENTER FIELDER...
SCHULZ

ARE YOU THE CATCHER?
OF COURSE, I'M THE CATCHER! WHAT ARE YOU DOING? WHAT ARE...
WAP!
NICE CATCH, "DEAR HEART"!
SCHULZ

I'M GOING TO TELL YOU SOMETHING I'VE NEVER TOLD ANYONE BEFORE...
DO YOU SEE THAT HILL OVER THERE?
SOMEDAY, I'M GOING TO GO OVER THAT HILL, AND FIND THE ANSWER TO MY DREAMS...
SOMEDAY I'M GOING TO GO OVER THAT HILL, AND FIND HAPPINESS AND FULFILLMENT...
I THINK THAT, FOR ME, ALL THE ANSWERS TO LIFE LIE BEYOND THOSE CLOUDS AND OVER THE GRASSY SLOPES OF THAT HILL!
PERHAPS THERE'S ANOTHER LITTLE KID ON THE OTHER SIDE OF THAT HILL WHO IS LOOKING THIS WAY AND THINKING THAT ALL THE ANSWERS TO LIFE LIE ON THIS SIDE OF THAT HILL...
FORGET IT, KID!
SCHULZ

"SEVENTH ANNUAL WORLD'S WRIST WRESTLING CHAMPIONSHIP"
YOU SHOULD ENTER, SNOOPY... IT'S GOING TO BE HELD ON MAY 3rd IN PETALUMA..
"PETALUMA"?
THE DEFENDING CHAMPION STANDS SIX FOOT THREE AND WEIGHS 333 POUNDS..
"PETALUMA"?!
SCHULZ

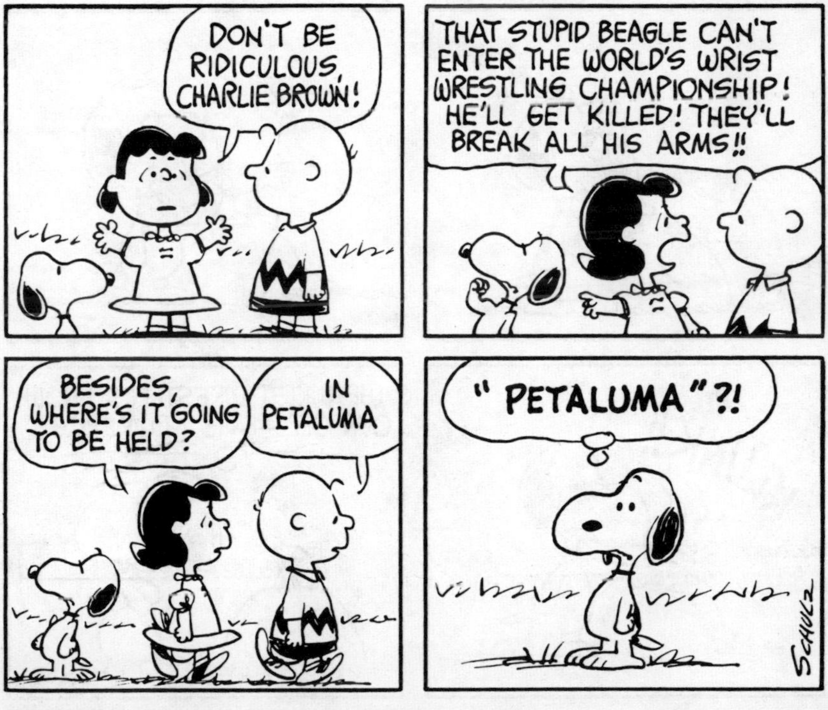
DON'T BE RIDICULOUS, CHARLIE BROWN!
THAT STUPID BEAGLE CAN'T ENTER THE WORLD'S WRIST WRESTLING CHAMPIONSHIP! HE'LL GET KILLED! THEY'LL BREAK ALL HIS ARMS!!
BESIDES, WHERE'S IT GOING TO BE HELD?
IN PETALUMA
"PETALUMA"?!
SCHULZ

HERE'S THE WORLD-FAMOUS WRIST WRESTLER TAKING PART IN A PRACTICE MATCH BEFORE HE GOES TO PETALUMA FOR THE CHAMPIONSHIPS...
WAM!
THERE'S FEAR AND TREMBLING IN PETALUMA TONIGHT!
SCHULZ

KLUNK!!
WE WRIST WRESTLERS SHOW OUR OPPONENTS NO MERCY!
SCHULZ

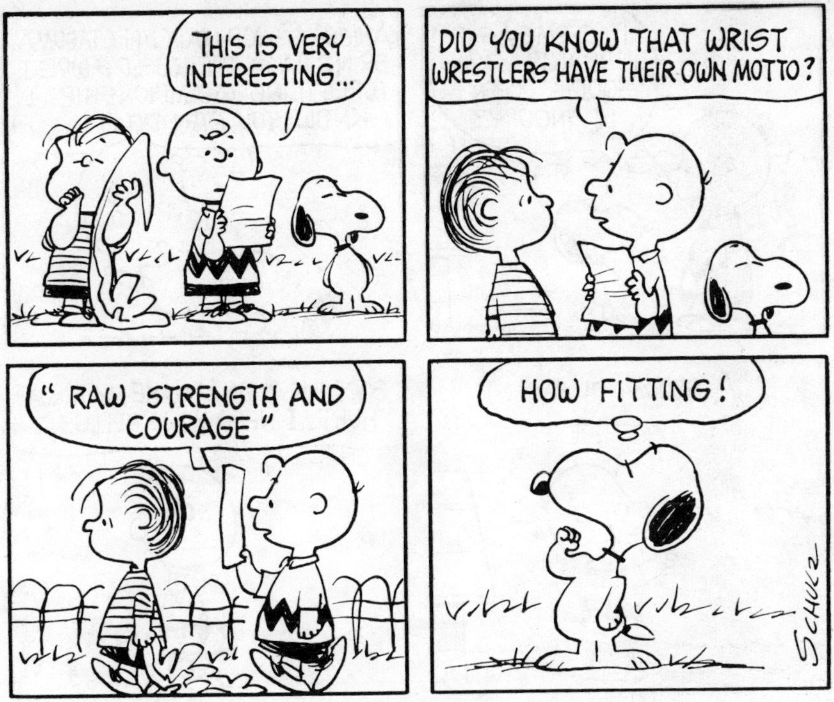
THIS IS VERY INTERESTING...
DID YOU KNOW THAT WRIST WRESTLERS HAVE THEIR OWN MOTTO?
" RAW STRENGTH AND COURAGE "
HOW FITTING!
SCHULZ

YOU STUPID BEAGLE, YOU CAN'T GO TO PETALUMA FOR THE WORLD'S WRIST WRESTLING CHAMPIONSHIP...
YOU'LL GET LOST OR FALL IN A HOLE OR SOMETHING!
IS THAT WHAT YOU WANT TO HAVE HAPPEN? YOU WANT TO GET LOST OR FALL IN A HOLE OR SOMETHING?!
STUPID BEAGLE!
SCHULZ

IT SEEMS AS IF WE'RE ALWAYS SAYING GOODBY, DOESN'T IT, SNOOPY?
ANYWAY, GOOD LUCK IN PETALUMA! BRING BACK THE WORLD'S WRIST WRESTLING CHAMPIONSHIP... I KNOW YOU CAN DO IT!
GOODBY, OL' PAL...
GOODBYS ALWAYS MAKE MY THROAT HURT... I NEED MORE HELLOS...
SCHULZ

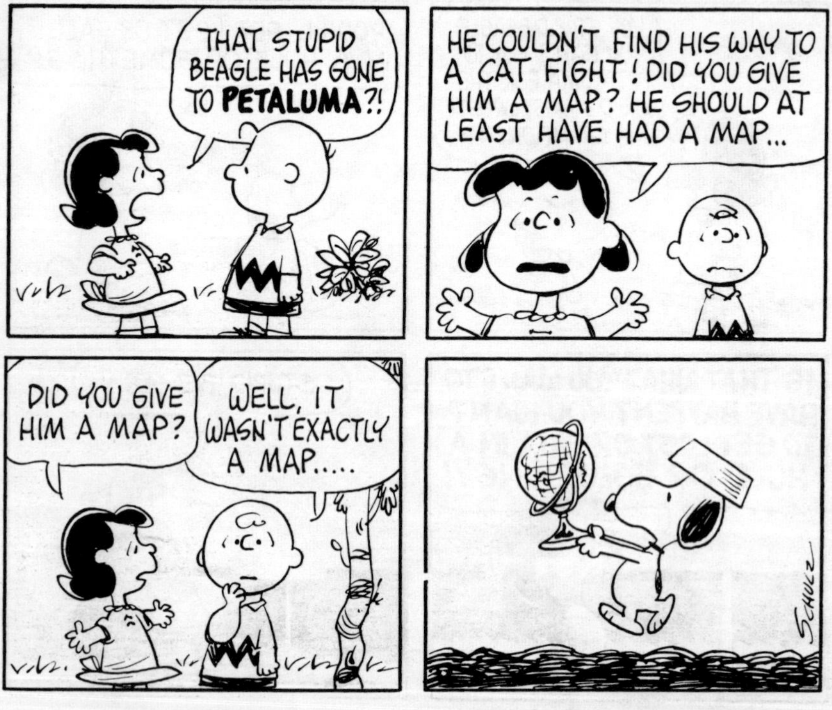
THAT STUPID BEAGLE HAS GONE TO **PETALUMA**?!
HE COULDN'T FIND HIS WAY TO A CAT FIGHT! DID YOU GIVE HIM A MAP? HE SHOULD AT LEAST HAVE HAD A MAP...
DID YOU GIVE HIM A MAP?
WELL, IT WASN'T EXACTLY A MAP.....
SCHULZ

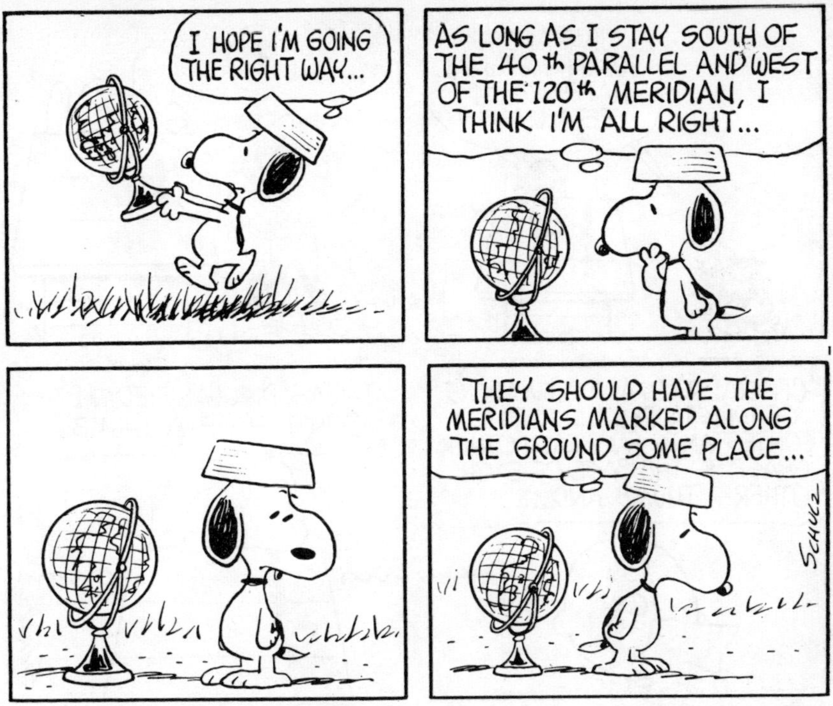
I HOPE I'M GOING THE RIGHT WAY...
AS LONG AS I STAY SOUTH OF THE 40th PARALLEL AND WEST OF THE 120th MERIDIAN, I THINK I'M ALL RIGHT...
THEY SHOULD HAVE THE MERIDIANS MARKED ALONG THE GROUND SOME PLACE...
SCHULZ

Welcome to Petaluma
Welcome to Petaluma
RATS! NO BAND!
SCHULZ

WHAT ARE YOU DOING HOME? WHAT HAPPENED IN PETALUMA?
?
"OFFICIAL RULES AND REGULATIONS OF WRIST WRESTLING... THE CONTESTANTS FACE EACH OTHER GRASPING THE BASE OF EACH OTHER'S THUMB AND...
I WAS DISQUALIFIED... I DON'T HAVE A THUMB!
SCHULZ

MOM PUT A NOTE IN MY LUNCH AGAIN, I SEE...
"DEAR SON, I HOPE YOU WILL STUDY HARD IN SUMMER SCHOOL.. DO NOT LOOK UPON IT AS A PUNISHMENT, BUT RATHER AS A PRIVILEGE..."
"WE ARE VERY PROUD OF YOU, AND WANT YOU TO HAVE A GOOD EDUCATION"
"THIS NOTE WILL SELF-DESTRUCT IN FIVE SECONDS!"
POOF!
SCHULZ

I HATE WINDY DAYS...
WIND IS VERY IMPORTANT... WITHOUT WIND OUR WORLD WOULD BE LIFELESS!
OUR OCEANS WOULD BECOME STAGNANT PONDS.. CLOUDS WOULD NOT MOVE.. FLAGS WOULD NOT FLY...
EARS WOULD NOT FLAP!
SCHULZ

I DON'T THINK MY TEACHER, MISS OTHMAR, LIKES ME ANY MORE..
SHE DOESN'T LOOK AT ME THE WAY SHE USED TO... SHE DOESN'T EVEN LOOK AT ME AT ALL...
IT'S A TERRIBLE THING TO DISCOVER THAT YOUR TEACHER DOESN'T LIKE YOU ANY MORE...
IT'S LIKE HAVING A SUBSCRIPTION RUN OUT..
SCHULZ

I'M GOING TO STAND HERE IN THE RAIN UNTIL I CATCH PNEUMONIA, AND DIE...
IF MISS OTHMAR DOESN'T LIKE ME ANY MORE, I HAVE NOTHING TO LIVE FOR!
I WONDER IF YOU CAN CATCH PNEUMONIA WITHOUT GETTING SO WET?
SCHULZ

WHAT ARE YOU DOING STANDING HERE IN THE RAIN?
MISS OTHMAR DOESN'T LIKE ME ANY MORE SO I'M GOING TO STAND HERE IN THE RAIN UNTIL I CATCH PNEUMONIA AND DIE!
HOW DO YOU KNOW MISS OTHMAR DOESN'T LIKE YOU ANY MORE?
SHE DOESN'T LOOK AT ME THE WAY SHE USED TO...
PLEASE MOVE YOUR UMBRELLA.. YOU'RE THROWING ME OFF SCHEDULE!
SCHULZ

I RAISED MY HAND, AND MISS OTHMAR LOOKED RIGHT THROUGH ME..
NOBODY CAN LOOK RIGHT THROUGH YOU BETTER THAN A TEACHER CAN LOOK RIGHT THROUGH YOU
WHEN A TEACHER LOOKS RIGHT THROUGH YOU, YOU KNOW YOU'VE BEEN LOOKED RIGHT THROUGH!
WHY DOES MISS OTHMAR LOOK RIGHT THROUGH ME?
SCHULZ

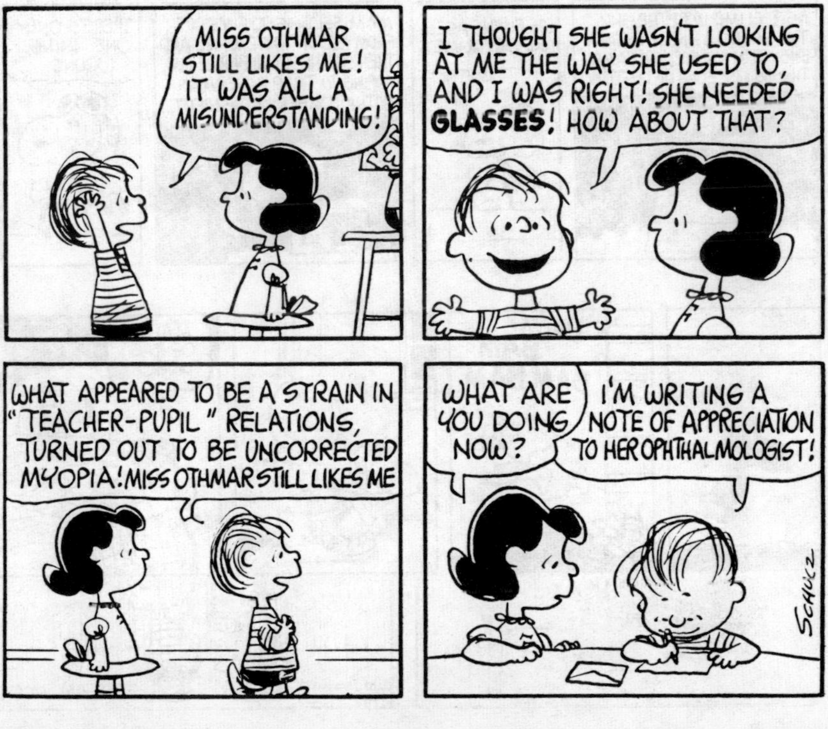
MISS OTHMAR STILL LIKES ME! IT WAS ALL A MISUNDERSTANDING!
I THOUGHT SHE WASN'T LOOKING AT ME THE WAY SHE USED TO, AND I WAS RIGHT! SHE NEEDED **GLASSES**! HOW ABOUT THAT?
WHAT APPEARED TO BE A STRAIN IN "TEACHER-PUPIL" RELATIONS, TURNED OUT TO BE UNCORRECTED MYOPIA! MISS OTHMAR STILL LIKES ME
WHAT ARE YOU DOING NOW?
I'M WRITING A NOTE OF APPRECIATION TO HER OPHTHALMOLOGIST!
SCHULZ

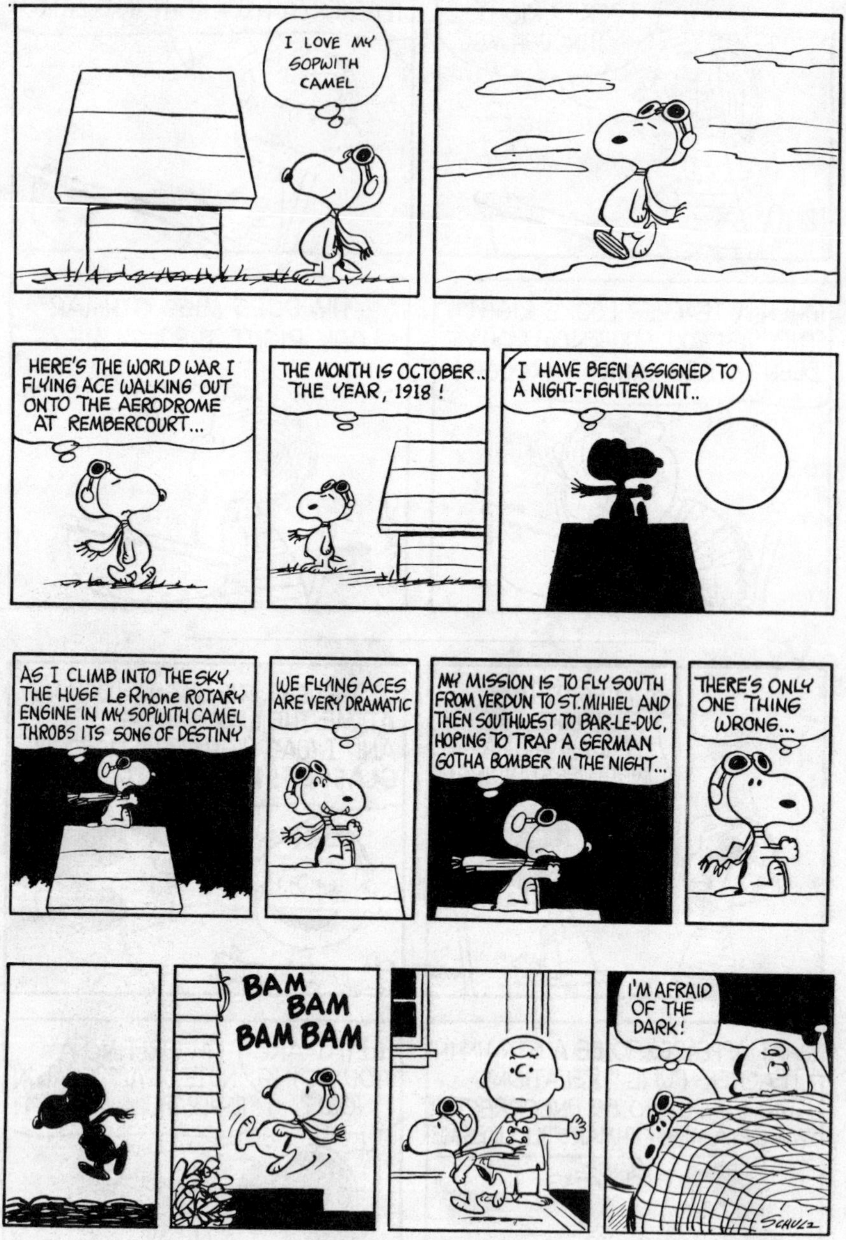
I LOVE MY SOPWITH CAMEL
HERE'S THE WORLD WAR I FLYING ACE WALKING OUT ONTO THE AERODROME AT REMBERCOURT...
THE MONTH IS OCTOBER.. THE YEAR, 1918 !
I HAVE BEEN ASSIGNED TO A NIGHT-FIGHTER UNIT..
AS I CLIMB INTO THE SKY, THE HUGE Le Rhone ROTARY ENGINE IN MY SOPWITH CAMEL THROBS ITS SONG OF DESTINY
WE FLYING ACES ARE VERY DRAMATIC
MY MISSION IS TO FLY SOUTH FROM VERDUN TO ST. MIHIEL AND THEN SOUTHWEST TO BAR-LE-DUC, HOPING TO TRAP A GERMAN GOTHA BOMBER IN THE NIGHT...
THERE'S ONLY ONE THING WRONG...
BAM BAM BAM BAM
I'M AFRAID OF THE DARK!
SCHULZ

DO YOU MIND IF I DUNK MY CHOCOLATE COOKIE IN YOUR MILK?
WHAT?
THANK YOU..
!
OOPS! IT BROKE...
AAUGH!
LOOK WHAT YOU'VE DONE! LOOK AT MY MILK!
I CAN'T DRINK THIS... IT'S SLUDGE!!
DON'T GET SO UPSET
WHAT DO YOU MEAN, DON'T GET SO UPSET?!
NEVER CRY OVER SLUDGED MILK!
SCHULZ

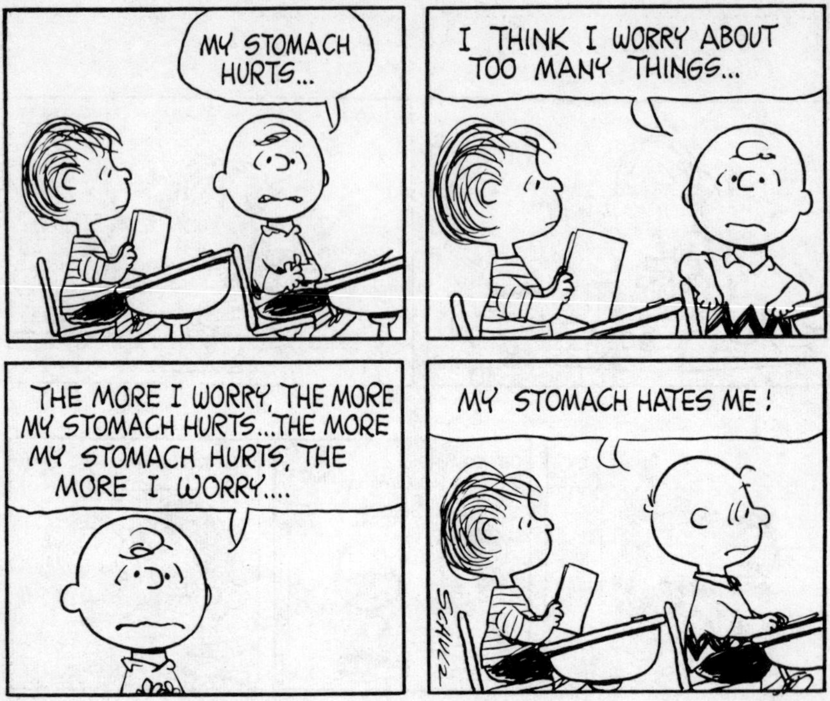
MY STOMACH HURTS...
I THINK I WORRY ABOUT TOO MANY THINGS...
THE MORE I WORRY, THE MORE MY STOMACH HURTS...THE MORE MY STOMACH HURTS, THE MORE I WORRY....
MY STOMACH HATES ME!
SCHULZ

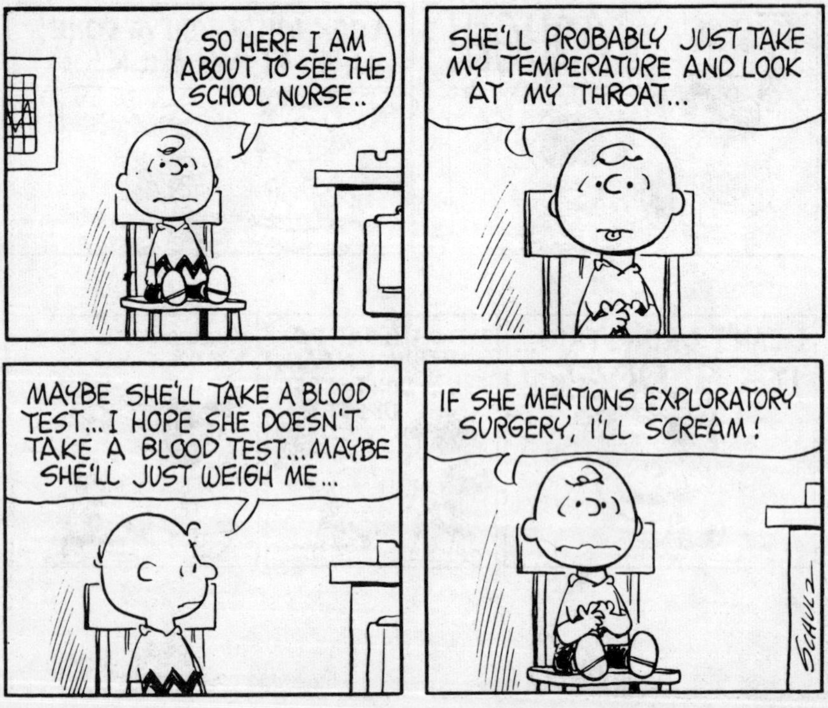
SO HERE I AM ABOUT TO SEE THE SCHOOL NURSE..
SHE'LL PROBABLY JUST TAKE MY TEMPERATURE AND LOOK AT MY THROAT...
MAYBE SHE'LL TAKE A BLOOD TEST...I HOPE SHE DOESN'T TAKE A BLOOD TEST...MAYBE SHE'LL JUST WEIGH ME...
IF SHE MENTIONS EXPLORATORY SURGERY, I'LL SCREAM!
SCHULZ

THE SCHOOL NURSE TOLD ME TO GO HOME UNTIL MY STOMACH FELT BETTER
I WISH IT WOULDN'T HURT ALL THE TIME...
OTHER PEOPLE'S STOMACHS DON'T HURT ALL THE TIME...
MAYBE I HAVE A CHEAP STOMACH!
SCHULZ

PSYCHIATRIC HELP 5¢
THE DOCTOR IS IN
I HAD TO GO TO THE SCHOOL NURSE YESTERDAY BECAUSE MY STOMACH HURT...
YOU WORRY TOO MUCH, CHARLIE BROWN... NO WONDER YOUR STOMACH HURTS... YOU'VE GOT TO STOP ALL THIS SILLY WORRYING!
HOW DO I STOP?
THE DOCTOR IS IN
THAT'S YOUR WORRY! FIVE CENTS, PLEASE!!
THE DOCTOR IS IN
SCHULZ

SNOW?!
BUT I'M NOT READY FOR WINTER!
MY BLOOD'S TOO THIN! I STILL HAVE MY SUMMER FUR!
STOP SNOWING! STOP IT, I SAY! STOP THIS STUPID SNOWING!
RATS!
SCHULZ

ALL RIGHT, SWITCH CHANNELS!
AND GET UP SO I CAN SIT THERE!
WHILE YOU'RE UP, GO INTO THE KITCHEN AND GET ME SOME ICE CREAM!
I'M SURPRISED THAT MY HAIR DOESN'T TURN GRAY..
SCHULZ

PAW POWER!
SCHULZ

I WOULDN'T VOTE FOR YOU IF YOU WERE THE LAST BEAGLE ON EARTH!
WAAH!
ALL RIGHT! IF YOU WERE THE LAST BEAGLE ON EARTH, I'D VOTE FOR YOU!
CAMPAIGN STRATEGY!
SCHULZ

I DON'T KNOW.. I'M NOT SURE IF I'LL VOTE FOR YOU OR NOT..
WAAH!
ALL RIGHT! ALL RIGHT! I'LL VOTE FOR YOU... STOP CRYING!
WHAT A SENSITIVE CANDIDATE!
SCHULZ

WAAH!
WHAT KIND OF A CANDIDATE IS THAT? IF YOU SAY YOU'RE NOT GOING TO VOTE FOR HIM, HE CRIES..
THAT ISN'T THE ONLY PROBLEM..
I DON'T EVEN KNOW WHAT OFFICE I'M RUNNING FOR!
SCHULZ

CAMPAIGN HEADQUARTERS
CAMPAIGN
KLUNK!
CAMPAIGN HEADQUARTERS
MY CAMPAIGN MANAGER ISN'T TOO BRIGHT!
CAMPAIGN HEADQUARTERS
SCHULZ

I THINK YOU'RE GOING ABOUT THIS ALL WRONG..
YOU'VE GOT TO DO MORE THAN JUST CARRY A SIGN
IF YOU'RE GOING TO GET ELECTED, YOU'RE GOING TO HAVE TO SHAKE A LOT OF HANDS AND KISS PEOPLE..
HOW GAUCHE!
SCHULZ

WHY SHOULD I VOTE FOR YOU?
I MEAN, CAN YOU GIVE ME A REASON?
IF I'M GOING TO VOTE FOR SOMEONE, I WANT TO HAVE A GOOD REASON..
WELL, FOR ONE THING, I'M KIND OF GROOVY!
SCHULZ

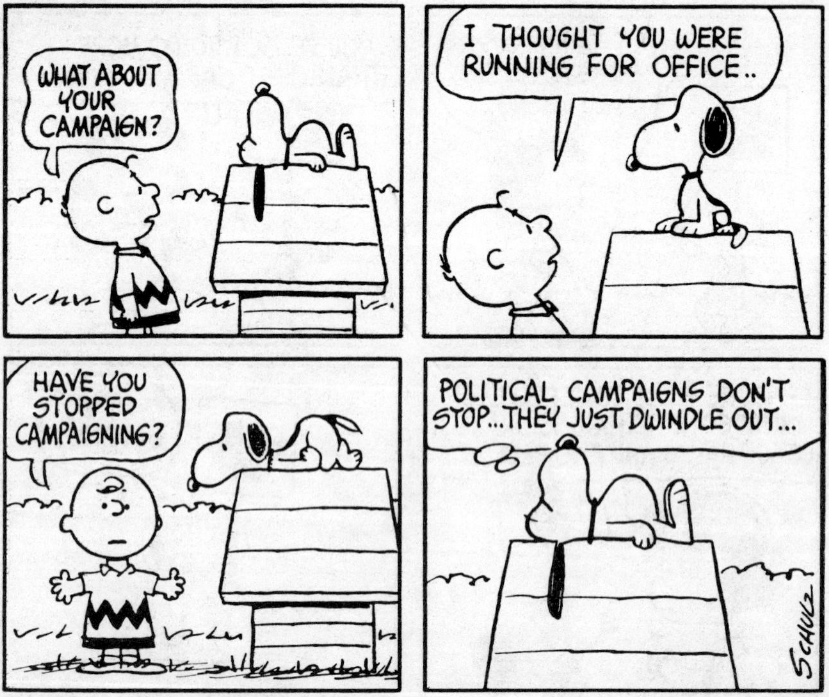
WHAT ABOUT YOUR CAMPAIGN?
I THOUGHT YOU WERE RUNNING FOR OFFICE..
HAVE YOU STOPPED CAMPAIGNING?
POLITICAL CAMPAIGNS DON'T STOP...THEY JUST DWINDLE OUT...
SCHULZ

I HEAR SOMEONE WALKING AROUND..
I KNEW I HEARD SOMEONE WALKING AROUND!
THERE'S A BUG IN MY SUPPER DISH...
HERE YOU ARE, SNOOPY...HERE'S YOUR SUPPER..
I WONDER IF HE TOOK THAT BUG OUT OF MY SUPPER DISH?
SURELY HE WOULDN'T JUST PLOP MY SUPPER RIGHT ON TOP OF A BUG..STILL, YOU NEVER KNOW....
BLEAH!
I DON'T WANT TO SWALLOW A STUPID BUG!
SURELY HE MUST HAVE SEEN THE BUG AND TIPPED HIM OUT... HE MUST HAVE..MUSTN'T HE?
I'M STARVING TO DEATH BECAUSE OF A STUPID BUG! MY SUPPER IS SITTING THERE, AND I'M STARVING TO DEATH, AND..
OH, INCIDENTALLY.. IF YOU'RE WORRIED ABOUT THAT BUG, I TIPPED HIM OUT
GOOD OL' CHARLIE BROWN!
SCHULZ

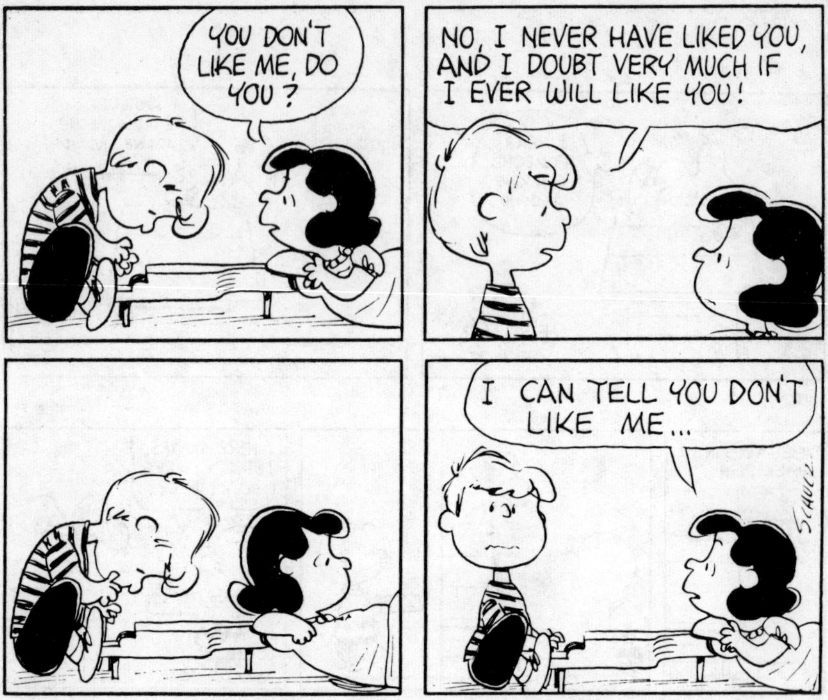
YOU DON'T LIKE ME, DO YOU ?
NO, I NEVER HAVE LIKED YOU, AND I DOUBT VERY MUCH IF I EVER WILL LIKE YOU !
I CAN TELL YOU DON'T LIKE ME...
SCHULZ

HERE I AM WALKING ACROSS THE AERODROME TO MY SOPWITH CAMEL..
THE WEATHER IS CLEAR... IT SHOULD BE A GOOD DAY...
MY MECHANIC LIKES TO PRETEND HE'S A WORLD WAR I FLYING ACE !
SCHULZ

WHAT?!
I CAN'T BELIEVE IT!
WHAT A BITTER BLOW..
MY MECHANIC HAS BEEN TRANSFERRED TO THE INFANTRY!
SCHULZ

?
TROMP TROMP TROMP TROMP
TROMP TROMP TROMP TROMP
TROMP TROMP TROMP TROMP
MY BUDDY, THE INFANTRYMAN!
SCHULZ

WHAT ARE YOU HANGING AROUND THE HOUSE FOR?
I'M AFRAID
AFRAID?!
I'M AFRAID TO GO OUTSIDE.. THERE'S A VULTURE SITTING ON MY SNOWMAN!
SEE?
WELL, HE WON'T BE SITTING THERE VERY LONG THE WAY THE SUN IS SHINING...
STUPID BEAGLE!
WE VULTURES HAVE A HARD LIFE...
SCHULZ

BUT FIFTY IS MORE THAN TWENTY-FIVE!
YOU SIMPLY DON'T UNDERSTAND DIVISION..NO WONDER YOU'VE BEEN GETTING SUCH POOR GRADES...
YOU CAN'T MAKE FIFTY GO INTO TWENTY-FIVE!
YOU CAN IF YOU PUSH IT!
SCHULZ

YOU KNOW, YOU AMAZE ME...YOU REALLY DO...
HERE YOU ARE, VIRTUALLY FAILING IN MATH, AND YOU DON'T SEEM TO CARE!
WHAT DO YOU MEAN, I DON'T CARE? OF COURSE, I CARE!
WELL, IT DOESN'T SEEM TO BOTHER YOU...
I TRY NOT TO TAKE IT PERSONALLY!
SCHULZ

HERE'S THE WORLD WAR I FLYING ACE ZOOMING THROUGH THE AIR IN HIS SOPWITH CAMEL..
OVER THERE! OVER THERE!
PACK UP YOUR TROUBLES IN YOUR OLD KIT BAG....
HOW IN THE WORLD AM I GOING TO GET MY TROUBLES IN A "KIT BAG"?
SCHULZ

HERE'S THE WORLD WAR I FLYING ACE STANDING BESIDE HIS SOPWITH CAMEL
IT IS EVENING... CHOW IS OVER... HE IS ENTERTAINING THE ENLISTED MEN WITH TALES OF BRAVE DUELS FOUGHT IN THE SKY...
POOR BLIGHTERS...THEY NEED INSPIRATION AND CHEERING UP...
BUT WHO CHEERS UP THE WORLD WAR I FLYING ACE?
SCHULZ

THAT'S GOOD EXERCISE!

THAT'S NOT ART!
THAT'S A TERRIBLE DRAWING! YOU HAVE ABSOLUTELY NO TALENT!
NO ONE EVER LISTENS TO US CRITICS...

SIGH!
CURSE THIS STUPID WAR!
HERE'S THE WORLD WAR I FLYING ACE SITTING ON HIS BUNK...HE IS DEPRESSED..
THIS WAR IS NEVER GOING TO END.. IT'S ALL MADNESS...IT'S INSANITY!
I NEED SOMEONE TO TALK TO..
PERHAPS ONE OF THE NURSES AT THE DISPENSARY WILL TALK WITH ME....
PSYCHIATRIC HELP 5¢
WELL! I WAS WONDERING HOW LONG IT WOULD BE BEFORE YOU CAME TO SEE ME...
THE DOCTOR IS IN
AH! A DARK-HAIRED LASS... QUITE A BEAUTY, TOO! IT'S GOOD TO SEE A FEMININE FACE...
IT'S JUST NOT NORMAL FOR A BEAGLE TO GO AROUND WEARING A FLYING HELMET..
IT'S HEART-WARMING TO THINK OF THESE AMERICAN GIRLS COMING CLEAR OVER HERE TO SERVE!
SNIF
THE FIRST THING WE HAVE TO DO IS TALK ABOUT HOW ALL THIS STARTED..
I THINK THIS LASS HAS FALLEN FOR ME ALREADY.. THE NEXT MOVE IS OBVIOUSLY MINE....... SHOULD I OR SHOULDN'T I? WHO KNOWS WHAT TOMORROW MAY BRING?
SMAK
ALL SOLDIERS SHOULD KISS AN ARMY NURSE AT LEAST ONCE IN THEIR LIVES!
SCHULZ

I KNOW WHAT'S ON YOUR MIND...
LET ME WARN YOU RIGHT NOW THAT FOR EVERY SNOWBALL YOU THROW AT ME, I'M GOING TO CLOBBER YOU WITH FIVE!
WAP!
POW! POW! POW! POW! POW!
WAP!
POW! POW! POW! POW! POW!!
WAP!
POW! POW! POW! POW! POW!
WAP!
POW! POW! POW! POW! POW!!
THE ODDS ARE KILLING ME!
SCHULZ

I HATE WINDY DAYS!
SCHULZ

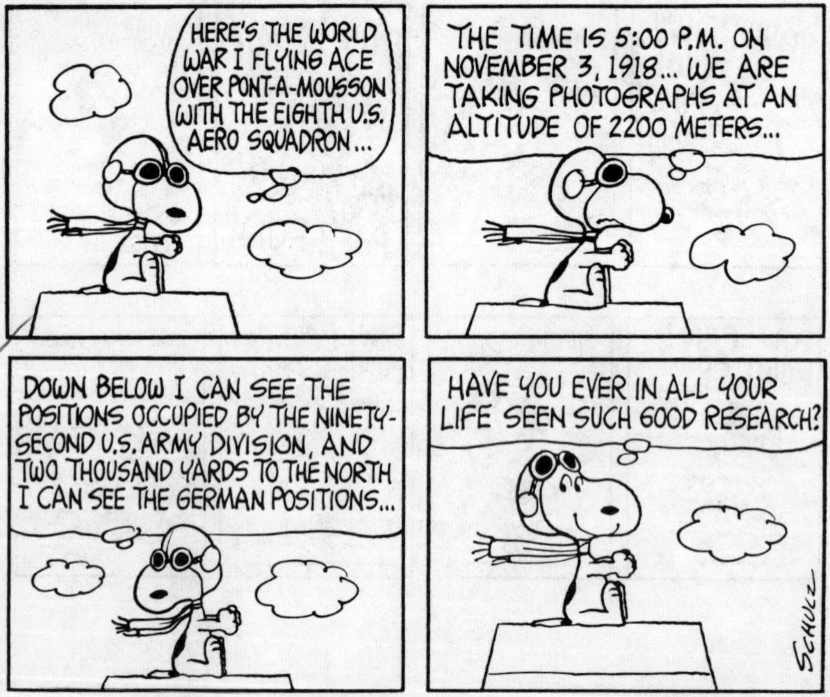
HERE'S THE WORLD WAR I FLYING ACE OVER PONT-A-MOUSSON WITH THE EIGHTH U.S. AERO SQUADRON...
THE TIME IS 5:00 P.M. ON NOVEMBER 3, 1918... WE ARE TAKING PHOTOGRAPHS AT AN ALTITUDE OF 2200 METERS...
DOWN BELOW I CAN SEE THE POSITIONS OCCUPIED BY THE NINETY-SECOND U.S. ARMY DIVISION, AND TWO THOUSAND YARDS TO THE NORTH I CAN SEE THE GERMAN POSITIONS...
HAVE YOU EVER IN ALL YOUR LIFE SEEN SUCH GOOD RESEARCH?
SCHULZ

PTUI!
I THOUGHT YOU WERE OUT THROWING SNOWBALLS..
NO, I WAS OUT **NOT** THROWING SNOWBALLS
SOMETIMES I DON'T UNDERSTAND YOU...
THERE ARE A LOT OF THINGS I DON'T UNDERSTAND MYSELF!
SCHULZ

I MISS SKATING WITH SONJA HENIE...
SCHULZ

HERE'S THE WORLD FAMOUS FIGURE SKATER PRACTICING HIS "OUTSIDE EIGHTS"
HE REALIZES THAT HE MUST PRACTICE DILIGENTLY IF HE IS TO WIN A GOLD MEDAL AT THE OLYMPICS...
ACTUALLY, VERY FEW BEAGLES ARE EVER INVITED TO THE OLYMPICS!
SCHULZ

REAL FIGURE SKATERS SMILE A LOT...
MAYBE JUST A PLEASANT GRIN WOULD BE BETTER..
SCHULZ

I HEAR YOU'RE PRACTICING FOR THE OLYMPICS...
DID YOU KNOW THEY'RE BEING HELD IN GRENOBLE, FRANCE?
DO YOU KNOW WHERE GRENOBLE IS?
I DON'T EVEN KNOW WHERE FRANCE IS!
SCHULZ

BEING A GOOD FIGURE SKATER IS HARD WORK
RIGHT NOW I'M PRACTICING MY "OUTSIDE FORWARD ROLL"
LATELY I'VE HAD TO DO MY PRACTICING AT NIGHT...
OTHERWISE I'M SURROUNDED BY FLOCKS OF ADMIRING GIRLS...
SCHULZ

SNOOPY, I'VE DECIDED TO TAKE UP A COLLECTION TO SEND YOU TO THE OLYMPICS..
AND JUST TO SHOW YOU HOW SINCERE I AM, I'M GOING TO START BY PUTTING IN A NICKEL.. WHAT DO YOU THINK OF THAT?
WHAH!
WE FIGURE SKATERS ARE VERY EMOTIONAL!
SCHULZ

HERE'S THE WORLD FAMOUS FIGURE SKATER PRACTICING FOR THE OLYMPICS IN GRENOBLE..
TODAY I'M WORKING ON MY "DOUBLE AXEL"
THEY'RE GOING TO LOVE ME IN GRENOBLE!
SCHULZ

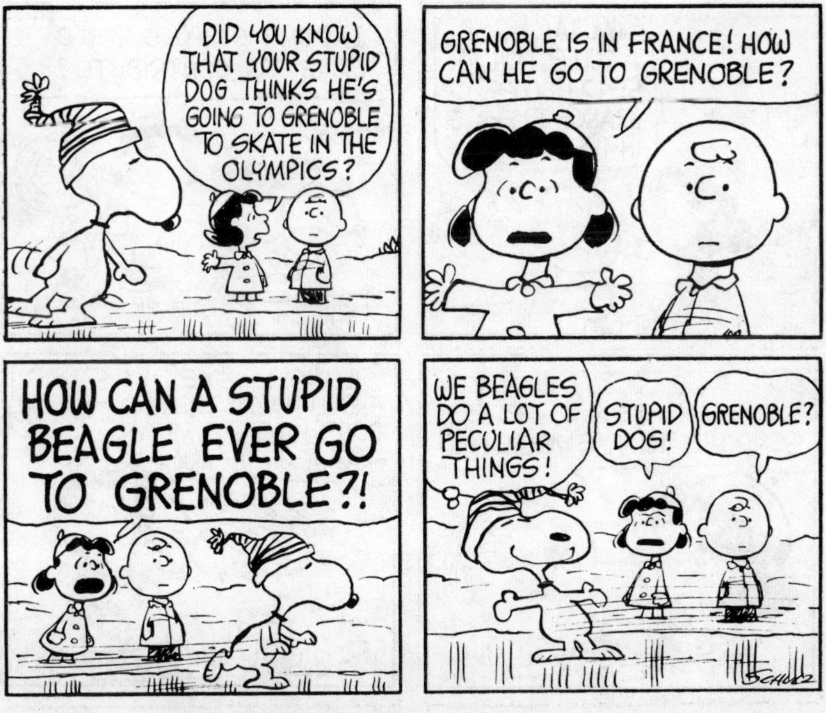
DID YOU KNOW THAT YOUR STUPID DOG THINKS HE'S GOING TO GRENOBLE TO SKATE IN THE OLYMPICS?
GRENOBLE IS IN FRANCE! HOW CAN HE GO TO GRENOBLE?
HOW CAN A STUPID BEAGLE EVER GO TO GRENOBLE?!
WE BEAGLES DO A LOT OF PECULIAR THINGS!
STUPID DOG!
GRENOBLE?

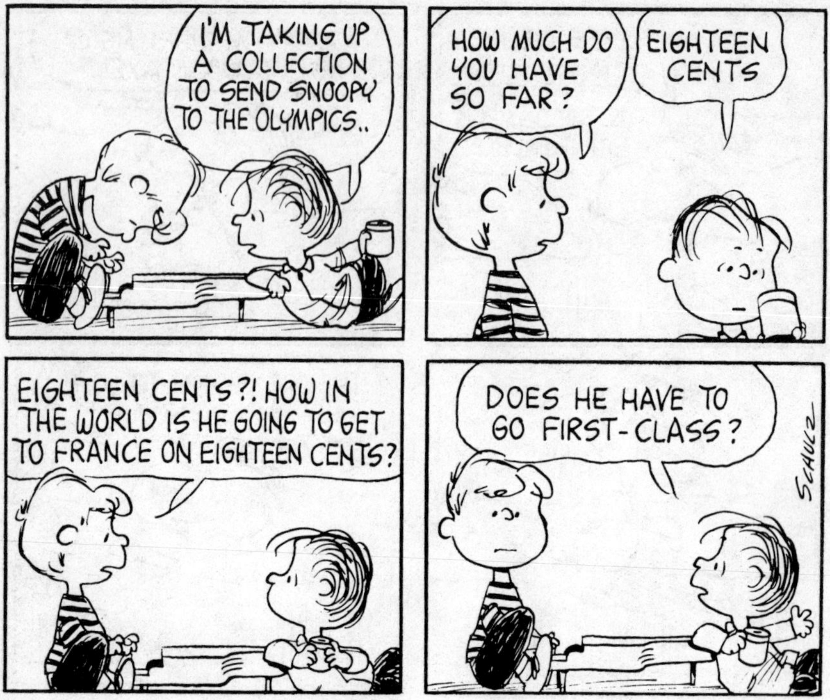
I'M TAKING UP A COLLECTION TO SEND SNOOPY TO THE OLYMPICS..
HOW MUCH DO YOU HAVE SO FAR?
EIGHTEEN CENTS
EIGHTEEN CENTS?! HOW IN THE WORLD IS HE GOING TO GET TO FRANCE ON EIGHTEEN CENTS?
DOES HE HAVE TO GO FIRST-CLASS?
SCHULZ

I'M TAKING UP A COLLECTION TO SEND SNOOPY TO FRANCE TO SKATE IN THE OLYMPICS..
I DON'T SUPPOSE YOU'D CARE TO CONTRIBUTE?
SURE, I WOULD, BUT WHY STOP THERE? HERE'S A QUARTER... SEND HIM TO THE **MOON**!!
SILLY GIRL...SHE SHOULD KNOW THEY DON'T HAVE FIGURE SKATING ON THE MOON
STUPID BEAGLE!!
SCHULZ

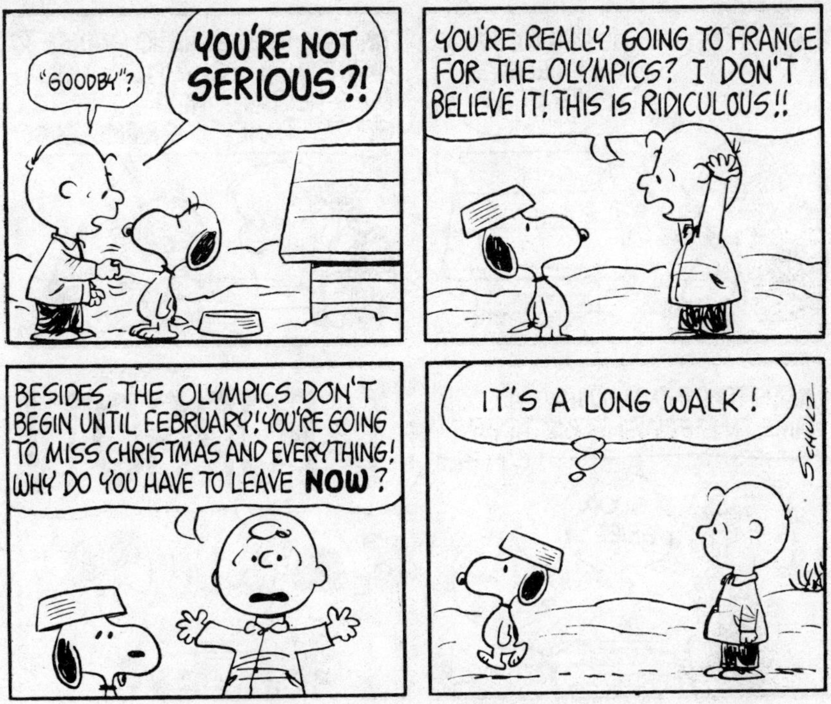
"GOODBY"?
YOU'RE NOT SERIOUS?!
YOU'RE REALLY GOING TO FRANCE FOR THE OLYMPICS? I DON'T BELIEVE IT! THIS IS RIDICULOUS!!
BESIDES, THE OLYMPICS DON'T BEGIN UNTIL FEBRUARY! YOU'RE GOING TO MISS CHRISTMAS AND EVERYTHING! WHY DO YOU HAVE TO LEAVE NOW?
IT'S A LONG WALK!
SCHULZ

THIS IS ALL YOUR FAULT! YOU WERE THE ONE WHO TOOK UP THAT COLLECTION!
NOW MY DOG HAS LEFT!! HE'S OFF SOMEWHERE WANDERING ACROSS THE COUNTRY! I'LL NEVER SEE HIM AGAIN! HE'S GONE!
BUT HE WANTED TO GO, CHARLIE BROWN! HE WANTED TO!
THAT'S RIDICULOUS! HE DOESN'T HAVE ANY IDEA WHAT HE'S DOING!
HERE'S THE WORLD-FAMOUS FIGURE SKATER ON HIS WAY TO FRANCE TO COMPETE IN THE OLYMPICS...
SCHULZ

HE'S GONE! I CAN'T BELIEVE IT! HE'S GONE!
MY DOG HAS GONE TO FRANCE TO SKATE IN THE OLYMPICS... HOW DOES HE THINK HE'S GOING TO GET TO FRANCE? IT'S RIDICULOUS!
INCIDENTALLY, DID YOU HAVE A GOOD TIME ON BEETHOVEN'S BIRTHDAY?
GOOD GRIEF...
I FORGOT!
SCHULZ

HELLO? I'D LIKE TO RUN AN AD IN YOUR PAPER, PLEASE
MY DOG IS GONE... WELL, I DON'T KNOW IF HE'S LOST OR NOT, BUT HE'S SURE GONE.... UH HUH...
WELL, HE'S MOSTLY WHITE WITH LONG BLACK EARS, AND HE'S GOT HIS SUPPER DISH ON HIS HEAD, AND HE'S ON HIS WAY TO.........
... BRACE YOURSELF, PLEASE... I JUST KNOW YOU'RE NOT GOING TO BELIEVE THIS...
SCHULZ

HOW CAN I ADDRESS CHRISTMAS CARDS WHEN I'M DEPRESSED?
HOW CAN I ENJOY CHRISTMAS WHEN MY DOG IS OUT WANDERING ACROSS THE COUNTRY SOMEWHERE?
SNIF!
HE MAY EVEN BE INJURED OR LOST OR STARVING OR MAYBE HE'S LOCKED UP SOME PLACE! OH, MY POOR DOG! MY POOR POOR DOG!
♪ IT'S A LONG WAY TO TIPPERARY.. ♫
SCHULZ

HERE'S THE WORLD-FAMOUS FIGURE SKATER ON HIS WAY TO FRANCE TO SKATE IN THE OLYMPICS..
NO ONE TOLD ME ANYTHING ABOUT AN OCEAN...
SCHULZ

MY DOG IS BACK!! HE'S BACK!
OH, IT'S GOING TO BE A MERRY CHRISTMAS AFTER ALL! MY DOG IS BACK!
WHEN DID HE COME BACK? WHAT HAPPENED?
I THOUGHT HE WAS ON HIS WAY TO GRENOBLE, FRANCE, TO SKATE IN THE OLYMPICS...WHAT MADE HIM DECIDE TO COME BACK?
WELL, THERE WAS THIS OCEAN, SEE....
SCHULZ

WELL, I DISCOVERED SOMETHING...
WHAT'S THAT?
YOU CAN'T AUTOGRAPH A SNOWBALL!
SCHULZ

?
HOW NICE OF HIM...HE JUST FLEW IN FROM GRENOBLE, AND HE SAID I WOULD HAVE WON EASILY!
SCHULZ

IF YOU SIT THERE MUCH LONGER, THE SNOW IS GOING TO COVER YOU UP!
CRAZY DOG!
I'M NOT CRAZY..
I'M JUST WITHDRAWING FROM THE WORLD!
SCHULZ

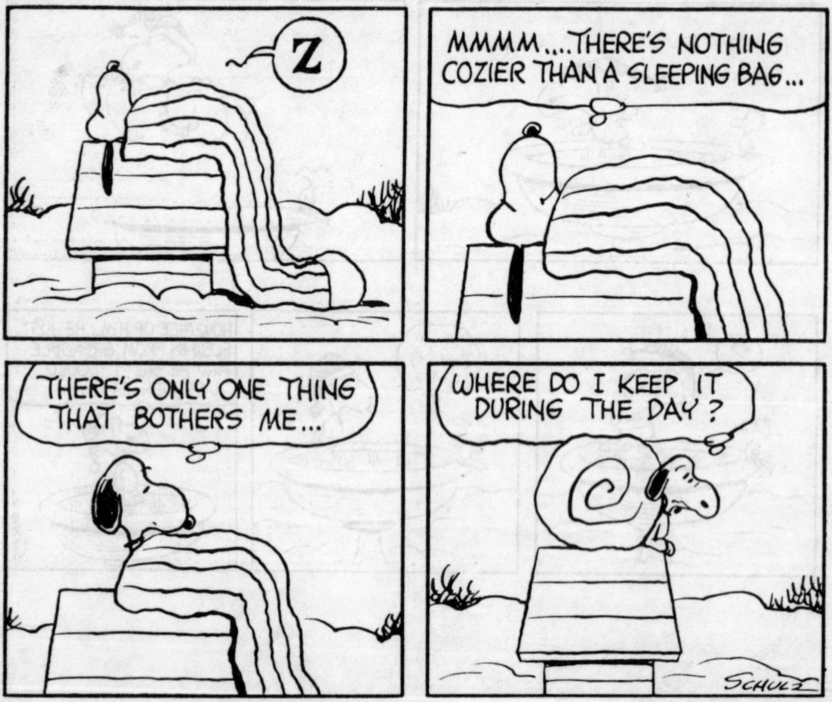
Z
MMMM....THERE'S NOTHING COZIER THAN A SLEEPING BAG...
THERE'S ONLY ONE THING THAT BOTHERS ME...
WHERE DO I KEEP IT DURING THE DAY?
SCHULZ

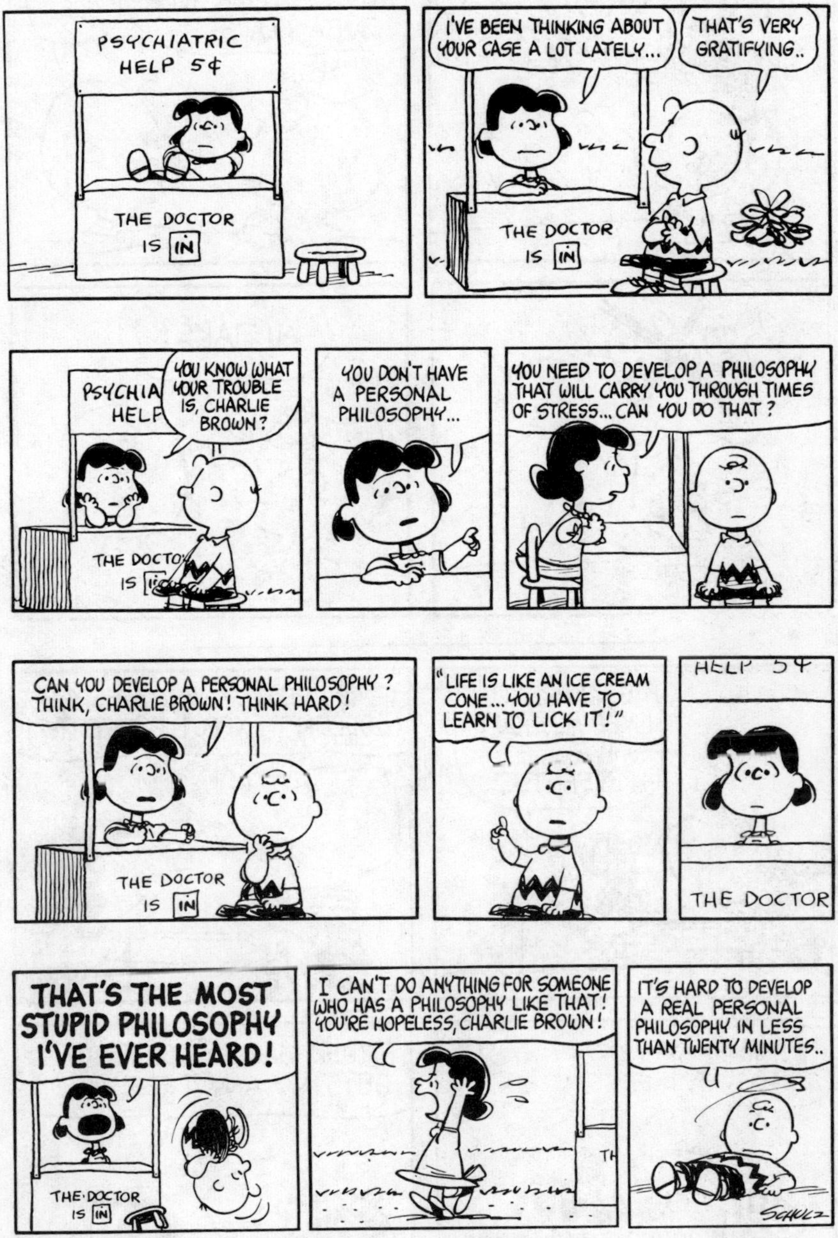
PSYCHIATRIC HELP 5¢
THE DOCTOR IS IN
I'VE BEEN THINKING ABOUT YOUR CASE A LOT LATELY...
THAT'S VERY GRATIFYING..
YOU KNOW WHAT YOUR TROUBLE IS, CHARLIE BROWN?
YOU DON'T HAVE A PERSONAL PHILOSOPHY...
YOU NEED TO DEVELOP A PHILOSOPHY THAT WILL CARRY YOU THROUGH TIMES OF STRESS... CAN YOU DO THAT?
CAN YOU DEVELOP A PERSONAL PHILOSOPHY? THINK, CHARLIE BROWN! THINK HARD!
"LIFE IS LIKE AN ICE CREAM CONE... YOU HAVE TO LEARN TO LICK IT!"
THAT'S THE MOST STUPID PHILOSOPHY I'VE EVER HEARD!
I CAN'T DO ANYTHING FOR SOMEONE WHO HAS A PHILOSOPHY LIKE THAT! YOU'RE HOPELESS, CHARLIE BROWN!
IT'S HARD TO DEVELOP A REAL PERSONAL PHILOSOPHY IN LESS THAN TWENTY MINUTES..
SCHULZ

I'M WRITING A LAST-MINUTE LETTER TO SANTA CLAUS...
I SEE..
MISTAKE!
SCHULZ

IF YOU REALLY LIKED ME, YOU'D GIVE ME PRESENTS..
IF YOU REALLY LIKED ME, YOU WOULDN'T EXPECT PRESENTS!
EITHER WAY, I END UP NOT GETTING ANY PRESENTS!
SCHULZ